"You're introspective. Every more than introspective; y about yourself a ridiculous an ‸ ‸ere is escape from suffocating in‸ ‸ nealing of the cataract of selfishness in your ‸ ‸i-eye. Let Jared Mellinger help you. He humbly and humorously speaks from experience. Discover, as Chesterton once said, 'how much larger your life would be if your self could become smaller in it.'"

Jon Bloom, Cofounder of Desiring God; author of *Not By Sight* and other books

"Jared Mellinger's book, *Think Again*, is simply one of the clearest, biblically faithful, most winsome, solidly helpful, and briefest(!) books you'll ever read on the topic of introspection. Jared skillfully avoids the extremes of never thinking about ourselves and always thinking about ourselves, and points us to the only cure for our self-absorbed souls: being overwhelmed by the matchless beauty and glory of Christ. I can't wait to give this to others."

Bob Kauflin, Director of Sovereign Grace Music; elder at Sovereign Grace Church, Louisville, KY; author of *Worship Matters* and *True Worshipers*

"In an age of narcissism, entitlement, and attention-seeking egos in search of self-esteem, we need more voices pointing us to a vision and story greater than self. For only when we lose ourselves do we find our truest, healthiest, and most life-giving selves in Jesus. Jared has written an excellent book to help us along in this journey."

Scott Sauls, Senior pastor of Christ Presbyterian Church, Nashville, TN; author of *Jesus Outside the Lines* and *Befriend*

"A self-absorbed culture keeps telling us that the solution to our problems is somewhere inside of us. So we keep looking. I talk about me, then I ask you to talk about me. More mirrors, more lanterns, more navel-gazing. Trouble is, these things aren't leading us to freedom and rest but to self-love or self-hatred. Jared offers us a way out of the vortex of introspection. Without obliterating the self, *Think Again* takes the reader up into worship and gratitude and out into the joy of service."

Matt Mason, Senior Pastor of The Church at Brook Hills, Birmingham, AL

"Introspection is a plague that cripples our souls and clouds the love of our Savior. *Think Again* addresses our daily temptation to focus our attention inward. Jared not only helps us discern this subtle tendency but also provides the liberating alternative in the gospel. This book delivers grace."

C. J. Mahaney, Sovereign Grace Church, Louisville, KY

"In this rich and thoughtful book, Jared Mellinger shows us that the solution to self-focus is God-intoxication. *Think Again* lifts the head of the introspective, the one lost in labyrinths of the self, and unveils the sure and certain hope of God. This God has not stayed silent; he has not kept to himself; he has not failed to provide a savior for sinners like us."

Owen Strachan, Author of *Risky Gospel* and *The Colson Way*; theology professor, Midwestern Seminary

"Martin Luther believed man's problem is that he is *incurvatus in se*—turned in on himself. In *Think Again* Jared Mellinger tackles one devastating effect of this in an astute, pastorally sensitive, and deeply searching but healing way.

Here is analysis, diagnosis and remedy all in one. Plus it's readable. The best books work on us while we are reading them and help effect the very transformation they describe. This is one of them."

Sinclair Ferguson, Author of *The Christian Life* and *Devoted to God*

"*Think Again* is a great little book. It navigates us through the maze of introspection in a biblical, practical, straight-forward manner. Read it for yourself; give it to a friend—for it shows how Christ can set us free from our own thoughts. I believe that for many people this will be a truly liberating book."

Tim Chester, Faculty member of Crosslands; author of over thirty books, including *You Can Change*

"*Think Again* is a surprisingly delightful book. Surprising in that such a short book can accomplish such depth in searching the reader's heart, delightful in its flow, humor, and encouragement. Jared, quite skillfully, delivers a very helpful resource for the very needed work of introspection. With great wisdom and the tender care of a pastor, Jared shepherds the reader to best see themselves only in view of Christ."

Brian Davis, Pastor of Risen Christ Fellowship, Philadelphia, PA

"Jared Mellinger understands that unless we learn how to take every thought captive, we can easily become captive ourselves to thoughts that control our emotions and ultimately, our lives. *Think Again* will help you find freedom as you learn how to guard your heart while renewing your mind."

Bob Lepine, Cohost of *FamilyLife Today*

THINK AGAIN

Relief from the Burden of Introspection

Jared Mellinger

New
Growth
Press
newgrowthpress.com

New Growth Press, Greensboro, NC 27401
Copyright © 2017 by Jared Mellinger

All rights reserved. No part of this publication may be repro-
duced, stored in a retrieval system, or transmitted in any form
by any means, electronic, mechanical, photocopy, recording, or
otherwise, without the prior permission of the publisher, except
as provided by USA copyright law.

Scripture quotations are taken from The Holy Bible, English
Standard Version.® Copyright © 2000; 2001 by Crossway
Bibles, a division of Good News Publishers. Used by permission.
All rights reserved.

Cover Design: Faceout Books, faceoutstudio.com

ISBN 978-1-942572-56-5 (Print)
ISBN 978-1-942572-54-1 (eBook)

Library of Congress Cataloging-in-Publication Data
Names: Mellinger, Jared, 1980- author.
Title: Think again : relief from the burden of introspection / Jared
  Mellinger.
Description: Greensboro, NC : New Growth Press, 2017. | Includes
  bibliographical references and index.
Identifiers: LCCN 2016054902 | ISBN 9781942572565 (trade
paper)
Subjects: LCSH: Introspection--Religious aspects--Christianity.
Classification: LCC BV4509.5 .M454 2017 | DDC 248.4--dc23
LC record available at https://lccn.loc.gov/2016054902

Contents

For the lovely Meghan Claire

Introduction

Do you ever think about yourself in ways that leave you weary and exhausted?

Welcome to the club. My name is Jared Mellinger, and I have been overdosing on introspection for as long as I can remember.

The goal of this book is to show how the gospel rescues us from fruitless self-examination, false guilt, discouragement, and inaccurate thoughts of ourselves. I want to offer practical counsel on battling unhealthy introspection and give hope to all of us whose minds are stuck on ourselves. Ultimately, I'm eager to draw our attention away from self and toward the glory of Jesus Christ.

Introspection is the act of looking inward. When we introspect, we are observing ourselves and reflecting on our thoughts, emotions, actions, and identity. Some of us are naturally more introspective than others, and this is certainly not a bad thing. The Bible commends self-examination and self-reflection.

But most of us lean toward extremes. Some people never study themselves; others constantly study themselves. I've written largely with those who tend toward hyper-introspection in view, but I hope everyone will benefit.

How do you know if this book is for you?

1. I've written to help those who know the burden of introspection, and who find themselves worn out from looking in.
2. I've written to help those who want to understand and care for others who experience the burden of introspection.
3. I've written to help all Christians discover how God wants us to think about ourselves.

Many of us are familiar with the problem of too much introspection. Our minds wander to our responsibilities, our spiritual growth, our appearance, or some other aspect of our lives. We spend excessive amounts of time evaluating ourselves. We overanalyze the things we say and do. We constantly second-guess ourselves and fear we might be making the wrong decisions in life.

In relationships, we are hypersensitive to the criticism and opinions of others. As employees, we fixate on our reputation and wonder what others are thinking and saying about us. We move through social settings with deep self-consciousness. We replay conversations in our minds.

As parents, we fear we are doing something (or *not* doing something) that will end up ruining our kids. We draw comparisons with other parents and their kids. On social media, we pursue the validation that comes from old), almost nine out of ten evangelical books published that year were on issues related to the self.[3]

David Wells has written at length about contemporary Christianity's enslavement to self. He explains that one shift that took place in recent decades has been moving away from thinking about human nature to thinking about the self.[4] Human nature consists of those things we all have in common. The self, on the other hand, consists of those things that are unique to each individual. The Self Movement idolized self and taught us that the most important things we need to know about ourselves are things unique to each of us.

This naturally leads to an endless study of ourselves and an introspective preoccupation with ourselves. As Wells says, "The downside of this self-worked therapy, of course, is that this constant taking of internal inventory only reinforces our natural self-centeredness and self-absorption."[5]

But Christianity teaches something different. We don't need to discover or know our unique, personal self as much as we need to learn human nature. Humankind has always been the same, and the Bible teaches us more about ourselves than we will ever learn by looking within.

John Calvin began his *Institutes of the Christian Religion* by affirming that "nearly all the wisdom we possess, that is to say, true and sound wisdom, consists of two parts: the knowledge of God and of ourselves."[6] Calvin was not encouraging an introspective, therapeutic knowledge of the inner self, nor saying that true wisdom is found in knowing everything that is unique to us individually. Rather, to be wise, we must know what the Bible teaches about human nature.

When Christians in the past talked about knowing ourselves, they were talking about knowing the nature of humanity. The following are the questions we must ask:

- What is the goal for which God created us?
- Who are we?
- Are we loved and valued?
- Why is humanity so broken?
- What is wrong with the human heart?
- What is our eternal destiny?

We gain this knowledge of ourselves not by looking inward, but by looking upward. Calvin says, "It is certain that man never achieves a clear knowledge of himself unless he has first looked upon God's face."[7] Elsewhere he says, "When we have seen God, then we begin to feel and know what we are."[8]

Thomas Chalmers and the Dark Room

In his introduction to William Guthrie's seventeenth-century work *The Christian's Great Interest*, Thomas Chalmers says that self-examination is like a dark room. Looking at ourselves is often useless, because we can't see accurately in the dark. We can't brighten up the room by straining our eyes, expending greater energy, or taking more time to stare into the darkness. We will never see ourselves clearly simply by focusing more on ourselves.

In Chalmers's words, "Now it is not by continuing to pore inwardly that we will shed a greater luster over the tablet of our own character, any more than we can enlighten the room in which we sit by the straining of our eyes towards the various articles which are therein distributed."[9] Rather, we need to go over to the window and open the curtains. The sunlight represents the great truths of God's Word, which illuminate the darkness. "When I sit in darkness, the LORD will be a light to me" (Micah 7:8). Chalmers observes, "If we derive no good from the work of self-examination, because we find that all is confusion and mistiness within, then let us go forth upon the truths which are without, and these will pour a flood of light into all the mazes and intricacies of the soul, and, at length, render that work easy, which before was impracticable."[10]

As we welcome the sunlight, we learn who we are, and the gospel informs every look at ourselves. We are then able to look inward, when needed, without the frustration and despair that so often accompanies self-reflection.

Seeing Ourselves in the Sunlight of the Cross

The most important things we need to know about ourselves are learned as we look away from ourselves to Christ. If all of the treasures of wisdom and knowledge are hidden in Christ (Colossians 2:2), it should be no surprise that what we must know of ourselves can be found by looking to Christ.

When we look to the cross, our focus should not be primarily on ourselves. Yet among the many treasures of knowledge we gain at the foot of the cross, one of them is the knowledge of who we are.

The world has pursued self-understanding by looking inward—but when we seek to discover ourselves by looking inside ourselves, we become lost in ourselves. God has destroyed the wisdom of the worldly wise. God has given us Christ crucified, who is the power of God and the wisdom of God.

Have you seen yourself in the sunlight of the cross? Have you learned who you are by looking to Christ? Consider what we see when we look to Christ.

In Christ we see our dignity.

Francis Schaeffer once received a letter from an atheist. The man asked Schaeffer, "What sense does it make for a man to give his son to the ants, to be killed by the ants, in order to save the ants?" He was suggesting that the gospel is senseless. Schaeffer says, "I replied that it makes no sense at all for a man to give his son to the ants, to be killed by the ants, in order to save the ants, because man as a personality is totally separated from the ants."[11] "Personality" here means the state of being a person. In other words, from the standpoint of personhood, man and ants have nothing in common.

But man and God do.

God is not only infinite; he is personal. Jesus would not become an ant to die for ants, or a worm to die for worms. He became a man to die for humans, and this is not a senseless or foolish act—precisely because we are made in the image of God, to know him and enjoy a relationship with him. In this sense, the incarnation and the death of Christ reaffirm the value of all men and women as those created in the image of God.

In Christ we see our sin.

Seeing Christ in his perfection leads us to a greater sense of our sinfulness. As God reveals his glory in the face of Christ, we worship him and cry out "Woe is me!" (Isaiah 6:5) and "God be merciful to me, a sinner!" (Luke 18:13).

It was your sin and mine that held him on the cross. The severity of our rebellion against God and the consequences of our sin are seen most clearly in the death of Christ. "The wages of sin is death" (Romans 6:23). And when Jesus hung on that old rugged cross, bearing God's wrath against sin and breathing his last, he displayed not only the depths of the Father's love for us—he also revealed what our sins deserve.

In Christ we see our new identity.

When we look only inward, we are likely to think that we are just as sinful as ever. We are tempted to believe that our sin defines us most deeply. But when we look to Christ, we see the one to whom we are united and our new identity in him. We see ourselves in Christ—dying in him and rising in him. I am not now what I once was! In 2 Corinthians 5:17, Paul writes, "If anyone is in Christ, he is a new creation. The old has passed away; behold, the new has come." We have been given a new life, a new status, a new power, a new ambition, a new destination.

At the center of who we are as Christians is not our remaining sin, but our newness in Christ. As Herman Ridderbos says, "The dominant viewpoint under which Paul views the Christian life is not the remaining temptation of the flesh, but the power of the Spirit conquering all sin."[12]

True self-knowledge and humility do not come primarily by looking inward, and they certainly don't come by comparing ourselves with others. We look outward and upward to Christ.

In Christ we see our value.

By value I mean glory and honor and beauty. These things are increasing in us because of the gospel. "Just as we have borne the image of the man of dust, we shall also bear the image of the man of heaven" (1 Corinthians 15:49). Even now, we are being transformed into that image from one degree of glory to another (2 Corinthians 3:18). Christ comes to create a new self in us, which is being renewed after the image of its creator (Colossians 3:10). Broken mirrors are being fixed. His love is making us lovely.

Though we now shine dimly, one day we will shine like the sun (Matthew 13:43). Jaws will drop, and all of creation will sing for joy at the revealing of the children of God (Romans 8:19). As Jonathan Edwards says, "In heaven, we will forever increase in beauty."[13]

The death our Savior died argues that Christians are deeply cherished by God and of great importance to him. Did Christ leave the presence of the Father for us? Did he willingly accept the punishment of sin for us? Then we know that the least and most sinful of God's children are of more value to him than anything in the world.

To be clear, we are not worthy of the least bit of kindness God has shown us. We should never think that God loved us because we are of such great value, in the sense that we are worthy or deserving of his love. That is anti-gospel and a lie. We are unworthy, but we are not worthless. Confusion comes in because we fail to distinguish between merit and value.

Even then, we find no value in ourselves apart from God. But he has loved us in his Son and has made the bride of Christ precious, honored, and valuable, like a most rare jewel. Being purchased by God at the great cost of the blood of his only Son makes the redeemed a treasured inheritance that we were not before. He now looks to us in Christ and says, "You are precious in my eyes, and honored, and I love you" (Isaiah 43:4).

We tend to base the way we feel about ourselves on our appearance, our performance, or how we measure up against others. We look for value inside ourselves, in our gifts and attainments. This produces fear and insecurity. But Christ reassures the children of God that we are more valuable than we know, and our value is grounded securely in the unchanging reality of being cared for, protected, and loved by our heavenly Father. "Are not two sparrows sold for a penny? And not one of them will fall to the ground apart from your Father. But even the hairs of your head are all numbered. Fear not, therefore; you are of more value than many sparrows" (Matthew 10:29–31).

In Christ we see our destiny.

Our deepest hope for the future is not discovered by looking at ourselves, but by looking to Christ. "Beloved, we are God's children now, and what we will be has not yet appeared; but we know that when he appears we shall be like him, because we shall see him as he is" (1 John 3:2).

The love of Christ for us secures our place among the bride, the wife of the Lamb, the holy city of Jerusalem that will one day be seen "coming down out of heaven from God, having the glory of God, its radiance like a most rare jewel, like a jasper, clear as crystal" (Revelation 21:10–11). When we see the judgment Christ endured on the cross, we are reminded of a future judgment. When we see his triumphant resurrection from the dead, we are reminded of a hope beyond the grave. In Christ and because of Christ, this is our bright future.

Looking to Jesus is not only how we learn who God is (John 14:9), and how we learn what love is (1 John 3:16), it is also how we learn who we are. We find ourselves in Christ alone. In this sense, it is the Christian alone who truly knows himself or herself.

By the grace of God, we are gaining a clearer view of ourselves as we learn to look away from ourselves and to welcome the sunlight.

Questions for Reflection and Discussion

- Why is it important for us to know ourselves?
- What does the cross of Christ say about who you are?

3
Selfie Sticks

Jesus is the end of self-hatred and self-esteem

I have to confess that the extent of my academic research on selfies is limited to Wikipedia, a website that is not exactly a bastion of reliability. Wikipedia itself—under the heading "We do not expect you to trust us"—says that "some articles [on our site] are of the highest quality of scholarship, others are admittedly complete rubbish."[1] Good to know.

Among Wikipedia's entries is one explaining the history of the term *selfie*, with links to some fascinating articles. (I'm not sure if this one is high-quality scholarship or rubbish.) One such article cites a study from 2013, stating that selfies account for 30 percent of pictures taken by those ages eighteen to twenty-four.[2] Many blast selfies as being inherently narcissistic, and when Oxford Dictionaries announced *selfie* as their word of the year in 2013, they said, "It could be argued that the use of the -ie suffix helps to turn an essentially narcissistic enterprise into something rather more endearing."[3]

Another article is titled "'Selfies' just as much for the insecure as show-offs."[4] The author notes that taking and posting selfies might not be as vain as it seems. Cultural and social media experts are cited, explaining that selfies are often just as much about reassurance and self-expression as they are about confidence and narcissism. And, sometimes a selfie serves the simple purpose of updating friends on our activities.

And then there is the "ugly selfie," discussed in an article by Rachel Hills, "Ugly Is the New Pretty: How Unattractive Selfies Took Over the Internet." Hills observes, "Posting intentionally unattractive selfies has also become common in the early 2010s—in part for their humor value, but in some cases also to explore issues of body image or as a reaction against the perceived narcissism or over-sexualization of typical selfies."[5]

I am intrigued by the selfie phenomenon because it touches on the issue of self-image. In the previous chapter, we considered the most important things we need to know about ourselves. Now, let's go a step further and consider how Christians are supposed to feel about ourselves—the question of self-image and self-perception.

The Question of Self-Image

Much of our unhealthy introspection occurs either because we are insecure and don't like who we are, or because we are consumed with our appearance.

We know something is wrong with the person routinely posting pouty, duckface selfies with the hashtags

"#Beautiful" and "#LoveYourself." It would appear, as author Joseph Epstein observed in the title of his book, that Narcissus has left the pool. But we also know that posting a gloomy picture with the hashtag "#Ugly" or "#IHateMyself" is no better.

Some would say that the answer is for everyone to stop taking selfies—and they might have a point. But the purpose of this chapter is not to bash selfies and selfie sticks. I'm interested in the idea of self-perception, and I want to consider what the Bible teaches about how we are to regard ourselves.

Our culture encourages a preoccupation with image and appearance. Social media feeds our excessive self-awareness. Overly introspective people often view themselves wrongly because they have made an idol of self. Our hearts restlessly pursue self-promotion, self-expression, and validation. And when we exalt the idol of self, we discover that self is a craving, merciless, and joyless god.

There is a light that shines in the darkness of our self-absorption and excessive introspection. What we learn is that the gospel rescues us from self-hatred and self-esteem by destroying the idol of self and replacing it with Christ.

The Idol of Self Has Failed Us

The idol of self has suffered a fate similar to the statue of Dagon in 1 Samuel 5. When the Philistines captured the Ark of the Covenant and set it beside Dagon, they awoke the next morning to find that Dagon had fallen face downward on the ground before the ark. So they took Dagon and put him back in his place. And when the people awoke the next morning, Dagon had once again fallen face downward, and the head of Dagon and both his hands were lying cut off on the floor.

This is what our culture continues to do with the idol of self. For decades we have set up the idol of self, only to find it toppling and crumbling to the floor again and again.

In 2012, *Harvard Business Review* published an article by Heidi Grant Halvorson entitled "To Succeed, Forget Self-Esteem." The article reported that at that time, there were already five thousand books on self-esteem under the self-help heading on Amazon. These books generally focus on why we need more self-esteem in order to succeed, and that the way to get ahead in life is to believe you are "perfectly awesome." Dr. Halvorson explains:

> And of course you must *be* perfectly awesome in order to keep believing that you are—so you live in quiet terror of making mistakes, and feel devastated when you do. Your only defense is to refocus your attention on all the things you do well, mentally stroking your own ego until it has forgotten this horrible episode of unawesomeness and moved on to something more satisfying.

When you think about it, this doesn't exactly sound like a recipe for success, does it? Indeed, recent reviews of the research on high self-esteem have come to the troubling conclusion that it's not all it's cracked up to be. High self-esteem does not predict better performance or greater success. And though people with high self-esteem do think they're more successful, objectively, they are not. High self-esteem does not make you a more effective leader, a more appealing lover, more likely to lead a healthy lifestyle, or more attractive and compelling in an interview. But if Stuart Smalley is wrong, and high self-esteem (along with daily affirmations of your own terrificness) is not the answer to all your problems, then what is?[6]

Once self is made an idol, I will either view myself as awesome or as a failure. If my standards for myself are low, I live life surpassing my expectations and I feel awesome. I am confident, self-assured, boastful, and look down on those who fail. If, on the other hand, my standards are high and I do not meet them, I feel like a failure. I am insecure; I feel worthless, unpresentable, and self-destructive.

Apart from Christ, and with self as our god, the only options are self-esteem (*"I'm awesome"*) or self-hatred (*"I'm worthless"*). The idol of self has failed us and cannot be the answer to our problems.

Narcissus and Dobby the House Elf

Narcissus, the character from Greek mythology, is a proud young man known for his good looks. As the myth goes, a nymph named Echo falls in love with him because of his beauty. She begins following him and shares her feelings with Narcissus. When Narcissus rejects her, Echo is heartbroken and dejected. She isolates herself in sorrow.

Nemesis, the god of revenge, determines she will make Narcissus pay. She lures him to a pool, where the self-obsessed Narcissus sees his own reflection. Thinking the reflection is another creature, he falls in love with it. Finally, he has met someone as good looking as himself. He is unable to take his eyes off of himself and is so in love with himself that he cannot leave the pool. He eventually drowns as a victim of his own self-love.

The character Narcissus is, of course, the origin of the word *narcissism*, which is a fixation with oneself and one's physical appearance. Narcissus is the epitome of self-love, self-esteem, and self-infatuation. Sadly, there are traces of narcissism in us all.

And then there's Dobby, the endearing house elf character in J. K. Rowling's Harry Potter series. He is helpful and loyal, but he regards himself as worthless (the "dregs of the magical world") and lacks self-respect. He constantly experiences unnecessary guilt. House elves are slaves, and Dobby has been badly mistreated by former owners. This abuse contributes to Dobby's inability to view himself as a complete individual, or as someone who has any dignity or worth. He treats himself as an object and as property that belongs to others.

Dobby is often cruel to himself. Whenever he speaks of his former masters, he has an impulse to hurt himself. His self-mutilation includes ironing his hands and shutting his ears in the oven door. At times, he intentionally bangs his head and yelps in pain. He regularly chides himself by saying "Bad Dobby, bad Dobby!" He refers to himself in the third person, not as "I" but as "Dobby." His speech reflects his loss of a sense of identity. Dobby is the epitome of self-hatred, self-abuse, and self-degradation.

Narcissus has a high degree of positive emotions directed toward himself and is a picture of inordinate self-love. Dobby has a high degree of negative emotions directed toward himself and is a picture of inordinate self-loathing. Both extremes are ultimately destructive.

How to Think of Yourself

In Romans 12:3, Paul says "For by the grace given me I say to everyone among you not to think of himself more highly than he ought to think, but to think with sober judgment, each according to the measure of faith God has assigned." There is a way to think rightly about yourself. It is the way of sober judgment, humility, and faith.

Jon Bloom wrote a helpful article entitled "Lay Aside the Weight of Low Self-Image." His main point is, "What our world often calls low self-image, I think Paul would say is just another way of thinking too highly of ourselves."[7]

Bloom observes that there are holy and unholy ways of thinking highly of yourself, and that there are holy and unholy ways of thinking lowly of yourself. *Correctly* thinking highly of yourself means knowing that you are created in God's image. We must know that we are adopted and loved by the Father who sings over us, we are sanctified in Christ who died and rose for us, and we are indwelt by the Holy Spirit who is a guarantee of our inheritance until we acquire possession of it. On the other hand, Narcissus demonstrates the proud, self-important, unholy way of thinking highly of yourself.

God's way to think lowly of yourself is to consider yourself the foremost of sinners and to consider others more important than yourself. "But," as Bloom observes, "if you suffer from a chronic sense of failure, underachievement, and shame because compared to others you just are not smart enough, competent enough, gifted enough, organized enough, educated enough, successful enough, rich enough, or prominent enough, that is almost always an unholy lowliness."[8]

Thinking of ourselves more highly than we ought is pride. But thinking of ourselves as worthless and hating ourselves is not to be mistaken for humility. If I compare myself to those I consider more gifted and better looking, feeling bad about myself becomes an expression of pride. If I consider myself as having no worth, I am standing in opposition to the biblical teaching regarding

God's creation. Both distorted views are based on the proud refusal to believe what God says about who we are.

The Idol-Destroying Power of the Gospel

Self-loathing attitudes cannot be overcome by replacing them with self-confident attitudes. The thought that I am not nearly as competent and gifted as other Christians cannot be replaced by the self-confidence of believing I am more competent and gifted than most Christians. If I feel like a spiritual loser, it doesn't help to make a list of reasons that I am a spiritual rock star. If I feel like a failure as a husband and father, the solution is not found in coming to terms with my awesomeness in the home. If I go through most social settings thinking I don't have anything good to say, the answer is not to start thinking that I have a lot of wise and insightful contributions to make.

"I am unattractive" cannot be driven out with "I am ridiculously good looking." "People probably think I am a really boring person" cannot be exchanged with "I sure do hope people realize how endlessly fascinating I am." The problem is that self is still at the center. The idol has not been displaced. And the harder we try to raise our self-esteem, the more introspective and self-conscious we become.

It is through the gospel alone that the idol of self is displaced, as Jesus silences our self-hatred and self-esteem. How does he do this? By joining us to himself. In Christ we gain a view of ourselves that is not based on anything in us, but on the work he has accomplished for us. Tim Keller tells us how we should view ourselves in light of the gospel.

> My self-view is not based on a view of myself as a moral achiever. In Christ I am *simul iustus et peccator*—simultaneously sinful and lost, yet accepted in Christ. I am so bad that he had to die for me and I am so loved that he was glad to die for me. This leads me to deep humility and confidence at the same time.[9]

Only when the idol of self is removed can the proud become humble and the insecure become confident.

When John the Baptist saw Jesus, he cried out, "Behold, the Lamb of God, who takes away the sin of the world!" (John 1:29). John says that it is Christ, not himself, who is the groom at the wedding (John 3:29). John didn't find joy in his status or in promoting himself. Rather, he says of Christ, "He must increase, but I must decrease" (John 3:30). John steps off the pedestal. He walks away from the spotlight. He snaps the selfie stick in half and points the camera at Christ.

When Christ is at the center, we are freed to praise God for who he has made us to be without falling into self-hatred or self-esteem. Psalm 139:14 does not say, "I feel good about myself, for I am fearfully and wonderfully made." It says, "*I praise you*, for I am fearfully and wonderfully made." The focus is on God. The praise is directed to God, and the idol of self has been displaced.

When you find that you don't like yourself and would rather be just about anyone else, or when you can't stop dwelling on the aspects of your personality, temperament, and appearance you don't like, or when you feel ugly and undesirable, look to the Lord who created you with hands of love. "Your hands have made and fashioned me" (Psalm 119:73). You can trust that the creator of the heavens and the earth knew exactly what he was doing when he made every part of you. His creative wisdom and power are revealed in all the works of his hands.

Those with high self-image enjoy the praise they receive and think, *I am awesome.* Those with low self-image often want to receive praise they are not receiving and think, *I am worthless.* But through the idol-destroying power of the gospel, "I am awesome" and "I am worthless" give way to "Lord, I will praise you."

Go to Christ and behold his glory. Let self-absorption give way to Christ-absorption. There is no joy to be found in higher self-esteem or daily affirmations of our own terrificness. Christ alone can satisfy. He must increase, but I must decrease.

Questions for Reflection and Discussion

- How does the idol of self show up in culture and in our lives?
- Do you identify more with inordinate self-love or inordinate self-loathing?

4

From Introspection to Christ-ospection

Reassessing the reasons we reflect on ourselves

In his book *The Scarlet Letter*, Nathaniel Hawthorne describes the inner troubles of a young Puritan minister named Arthur Dimmesdale. Dimmesdale had secretly committed adultery with Hester Prynne, causing the woman to wear the red letter "A" that marked her as an adulterous woman.

There is grace in Christ for adulterers and for sinners of every kind. But Dimmesdale does not look upward to Christ, nor confess his sin to God and others. Instead, he looks inward. He hides his sin, internalizing his guilt and shame. Over time, his spiritual and physical condition deteriorates. His morbid introspection does more to ruin his life than the adultery itself.

Dimmesdale is a learned man, but his brilliant mind cannot think its way to peace. He regrets his actions, but his penance and grief is not enough to bring comfort. He is a religious man, but his fasting and his lengthy vigils that last through the night only bring more darkness to his soul. His tragic self-hatred and physical abuse of himself also fail to lighten his burden of guilt. He wants to confess the truth, but instead torments himself with endless self-reflection and meditation on his sin.

All of these empty remedies fail because they never move beyond an inward focus, and they leave Christ and his cleansing grace entirely out of the picture.

Hawthorne says of Dimmesdale, "He thus typified the constant introspection wherewith he tortured, but could not purify, himself."[1] This constant introspection, Hawthorne observes, "steals the pith and substance out of whatever realities there are around us, and which were meant by Heaven to be the spirit's joy and nutriment."[2]

There is a kind of introspection that sucks the life out of our souls. It steals the joy God intends for us to receive through knowing him. It blinds us to the beautiful realities of the world God has made and numbs us to the generosity of his many good gifts. It can torture us, but it cannot purify us.

Why We Introspect

There are times when we must look at ourselves. But healthy self-knowledge and occasional self-examination are much different than an introspective orientation to life. Our problem is not that we sometimes think about ourselves, but that we become consumed with ourselves.

To move from a life of introspection to a life of Christ-ospection, we need to understand the various reasons we are inclined to look inward and determine whether or not they are beneficial.

A desire to honor God

One reason we look inward is because we know it is a necessary part of the Christian life. God calls us to examine and test ourselves (2 Corinthians 13:5), to examine our ways (Lamentations 3:40), to keep a close watch on ourselves (1 Timothy 4:16), to keep our hearts with all vigilance (Proverbs 4:23), to look carefully how we live (Ephesians 5:15), and to not think of ourselves more highly than we ought (Romans 12:3). These commands cannot possibly be obeyed through total self-forgetfulness.

Additionally, you cannot listen to your conscience or enjoy assurance of faith without some degree of self-awareness. Likewise, we cannot receive in faith those statements about who we now are in Christ without thinking about ourselves in some way.

As Christians, we greatly desire our lives to honor the God who has saved us. Therefore, we take the commands to examine and watch ourselves seriously. As a result, many Christians tend to be self-reflective, even to a fault. We end up looking at ourselves more than we look at Christ. We struggle to apply the commands to examine ourselves without becoming discouraged. But often the impulse that first turns us inward is the right one. We have a noble desire to honor God through biblical self-examination.

An introverted personality

Temperament is not what defines us most deeply, but understanding our temperament can help us understand some of the temptations and inward struggles we might face. Personality plays a factor in how much we are inclined to think about ourselves. Introverts are naturally self-reflective and contemplative. In social settings, we are more likely to be shy and self-conscious. We are more energized by solitude than by crowds. We can feel like there is simply not enough time in the day to think about everything that needs to be mentally processed.

Being an introvert is not a curse. It doesn't mean you are a self-absorbed person. It might mean that you are vulnerable to excessive and unhealthy introspection, but you probably already know that about yourself. Don't despise your God-given personality. The world would be a terrible place if everyone were an extrovert. Granted, some people are able to go through life without struggling at all with excessive introspection. But those are the same people who would likely benefit from a bit healthier self-awareness, which is a strength God has given the introvert.

The pursuit of peace and joy

During the time I was writing this book, I read a good number of popular books related to self. Some were Christian; some were not. (Don't tell anyone, but I even read a couple of books aimed at helping women learn to love and appreciate themselves. All I remember is that I was told to look in the mirror and tell myself that I am "drop-dead gorgeous" and that every part of me is "stunningly beautiful." I am still not quite sure what to do with that counsel.)

The world claims that true satisfaction in life is found in viewing ourselves a certain way. The secret to a life of peace and joy, they say, is appreciating your significance and coming to terms with just how amazing you are. The Self Movement has continued to plow full steam ahead for several decades. It was fun while it lasted, but the movement is seriously misguided and places self on a throne where only Christ belongs.

The goal of the gospel is not to make me feel good about myself. The secret to happiness is not found in our view of ourselves; it is found in our view of Christ. Fullness of joy and pleasures forevermore will never be found through introspection. Self-revelation is not an end in itself. We do not long to behold *self*; we long to behold God. We do not pant as the deer for the flowing streams of self-knowledge; we thirst for the knowledge of Christ. Jesus does not pray that we would see our glory, but that we would see *his* glory (John 17:24).

If Jesus's invitation to all who are weary and burdened were "Look within yourself," it would hardly be a message of grace. Instead he says, "Come to me" (Matthew 11:28). The psalmist frequently looks away from himself and to the Lord for mercy and help in time of need: "To you I lift up my eyes, O you who are enthroned in the heavens!" (Psalm 123:1). The Christian's boast is not that we understand and know ourselves; it is that we understand and know the Lord (Jeremiah 9:24).

Dwelling on our sin

We have an enemy named Satan who accuses us day and night (Revelation 12:10). His first strategy is to prevent us from seeing our sin at all. But if he cannot keep us from seeing our sin, he will work to have us see nothing but our sin. He wants to leave us as he left the Puritan Arthur Dimmesdale—lost in regret, self-condemnation, and morbid introspection.

The Puritans are sometimes portrayed as if this is a weakness in their theology and practice in general, but it is more of a caricature than an accurate likeness. J. I. Packer says, "Morbidity and introspectiveness, the gloomy self-absorption of the man who can never look away from himself, is bad puritanism; the puritans themselves condemned it repeatedly."[3] Still, the reason we must condemn morbid introspection and gloomy self-absorption in every generation is because the condition is so common among believers.

The Puritan Thomas Hooker observed that one of Satan's strategies for keeping us in sin is by leading us to dwell excessively on our sin. The devil's lie is that the more we focus on sin, the more we will be free from it.[4] But ruminating too long upon our ruin is not a virtue. The Spirit's goal in showing us our sin is to drive us to Christ and the sufficiency of his grace. The reason we look inward is so we know what to look to Christ for.[5] It is not much use if we are experts in identifying sin, only to be novices at applying grace.

Sometimes we think that if only we can identify the bottom of our sin, if only we can gain enough insight into the idols of our hearts, *then* we will experience change. So we turn our motives over in our minds, examining every potential root and expression of sin in our attempt to escape our sin. This often results in confusion and condemnation rather than growth and grace. John Newton says, "It is better for you and me to be admiring the compassion and fullness of grace that is in our Saviour, than to dwell and pore too much upon our own poverty and vileness."[6]

Seeking the cause of suffering

This is similar to the previous point. But here, instead of dwelling on a particular sin, we look inward to order to discover a sin or fault that has caused our suffering. We wrongly assume that our suffering is always the result of our sin, and that hardship comes our way because our character is deficient or because we value something too much.

In John 9, the disciples of Jesus see a man blind from birth, and they ask Jesus, "Rabbi, who sinned, this man or his parents, that he was born blind?" (John 9:2). Their assumption was that suffering is always caused by character deficiencies. Job's friends had that same assumption regarding his suffering, yet Job was godlier than his friends and was described by God as a blameless and upright man.

Most often we suffer not because of some fault in ourselves that we must discover, but because we live in a fallen world and because we are united to Christ in his suffering for the purpose of glorifying the Father.

The pride of self-absorption

The main reason I look inward is the self-centered nature of sin. Self-absorption is not always loud and self-promoting; it can also look shy and insecure. It does not always come in the form of thinking of ourselves more *highly* than we ought. It also comes in the form of thinking of ourselves more *often* than we ought.

Second Timothy 3:1–5 describes what we once were: lovers of self, proud, arrogant, ungrateful, without self-control, and swollen with conceit. We still feel the inward pull of sin every day. However, the center of our identity is no longer *lovers of self,* but *lovers of Christ.* The grace of our Lord frees us from slavery to self-absorption and instead gives us a childlike trust in God, gratitude for his many gifts, a spirit of power and love and self-control, and a humble estimation of ourselves.

These categories reveal that there is both good and bad introspection. It is healthy to look inward from a desire to honor God, or even as a function of our personality. Yet we must introspect with caution, recognizing and resisting the tendency to self-absorption. And we need to keep in mind that there is something far better than a life focused on self.

The Self-Emptied Life

It is one of the most beautiful aspects of the life of Christ that he did not live consumed with his own will, governed by his emotions, preoccupied with what most pleased him, or fixated upon his own interests. "Christ did not please himself" (Romans 15:3). He says, "I seek not my own will but the will of him who sent me" (John 5:30). His life of humility and love reveals the joy of focusing on the Father and loving others. His earthly life and sacrificial death reveal the blessing of being free from self-absorption, and they blaze a trail for us to follow.

There is a lot of joy to be found in life by thinking about ourselves less often. The self-emptied life is a life of childlike faith and wonder; it is the opposite of a self-absorbed life. Discover the freedom of escaping condemnation, of removing the daily burden of false guilt, of avoiding the snare of the fear of man and the unhelpful comparisons that constantly trip us up.

Self-absorption is not only an ungodly quality; it is also an unattractive quality. We know this when we see it in others. Those who are externally good looking can become quite unattractive through their self-absorption. Those who are full of self will soon be empty of beauty. The opposite is also true. There is something appealing about a soul that delights in the Lord, serves others gladly, laughs at the days to come, and thinks far less often about how everything relates to self. This is who God made us to be.

When we think about ourselves less, we experience the blessing of greater usefulness to others. Our eyes are opened to opportunities to be generous, loving, and merciful to those in need. We gain more confidence in our roles—whether in marriage, as parents, as singles, in the workplace, or in ministry and service.

It might seem counterintuitive, but we actually gain a healthier view of ourselves by thinking about ourselves less often. Most importantly, taking our eyes off ourselves frees us to look up and treasure Jesus Christ, the Prince of Glory.

From Where Does My Help Come?

It's no wonder Charles Spurgeon says, "We must use our eyes with resolution, for they will not go upward to the Lord of themselves, but they incline to look downward, or inward, or anywhere but to the Lord: let it be our firm resolve that the heavenward glance shall not be lacking. . . . Let us look up, and so turn our eyes from too much introspection."[7]

Similarly, J. C. Ryle says,

> Cultivate the habit of fixing your eye more simply on Jesus Christ, and try to know more of the fullness there is laid up in Him for every one of His believing people. Do not be always pouring down over the imperfections of your own heart, and dissecting your own besetting sins. Look up. Look more to your risen Head

in heaven, and try to realize more than you do that the Lord Jesus not only died for you, but that He also rose again, and that He is ever living at God's right hand as your Priest, your Advocate, and your Almighty Friend.[8]

The psalmist says, "I lift up my eyes to the hills. From where does my help come? My help comes from the LORD, who made heaven and earth" (Psalm 121:1–2). Our help does not come from within, from discovering ourselves or believing in ourselves. Our help comes from the Lord Jesus Christ. We can find a lot of problems by looking inside ourselves, but we're not going to find solutions there. Self-help is a monstrous oxymoron. We cannot help ourselves; we need help from outside.

Where will you look today? Where does your help come from? Introspection is a lousy savior. We are far better off looking upward.

Questions for Reflection and Discussion

- Among the reasons we look inward, which do you most identify with?
- What does Christ teach us about the blessing of a self-emptied life?

5
Escaping the Dungeon

Breaking free from introspective doubt and despair

John Bunyan wrote his famous allegory, *Pilgrim's Progress*, to explain the nature and trials of the Christian life. Christian travels with his friend named Hopeful. One night they sleep on the grounds of a castle, only to be found by Giant Despair. The Giant takes them captive and leads them to Doubting Castle. They are forced to go along because Despair is stronger than they are.

Giant Despair keeps his prisoners in a dark and gloomy dungeon for several days. He beats them with a club, and from the Wednesday of their capture until Sunday, Christian and Hopeful are bound by introspective doubts and despair. Despair's strategy is to trap them in self-preoccupation and self-condemnation. He causes them to think of nothing other than their sins, their mistakes, and the misery of their condition.

The power of despair lies in its ability to trap us and bludgeon us. It overpowers us and takes us captive. It blindfolds us to the truth of the gospel, turns us inward, and leads us into spiritual depression.

Does Giant Despair have the upper hand in your life? Are you in distress? God wants you to know there is a way of escape from that dungeon. Jesus Christ has died and now lives to deliver us from our distress. His light shines into our darkness, and the darkness simply doesn't stand a chance of overcoming it. Christ bursts our bonds apart; he leads us out of the darkest night of the soul.

This doesn't mean we never experience darkness, discouragement, and despair. But it does mean, as the Puritan Richard Sibbes says, that the depths of our misery can never fall below the depths of God's mercy.[1]

Let's take a closer look at what to do when we feel stuck in introspective doubt and despair.

"My Soul Refuses to Be Comforted"

There is a psalm for every condition of the soul, which is one reason we should go to the book of Psalms in our distress. Asaph wrote Psalms 73–83. From what we gather through his songs, Asaph was not your typical, enthusiastic, extroverted, rock-star worship leader. He was clearly well-acquainted with depression, introspection, and melancholy.

Psalm 77 begins with Asaph experiencing the burden of introspection. There is unrest in his soul as he dwells upon his situation and his troubles. He tries to think his way out of his condition, but the more he meditates, the more miserable he becomes.

I cry aloud to God,
aloud to God, and he will hear me.
In the day of my trouble I seek the Lord;
in the night my hand is stretched out without
wearying;
my soul refuses to be comforted.
When I remember God, I moan;
when I meditate, my spirit faints. (Psalm 77:1–3)

There are times when we seek God, but our minds remain filled with cold thoughts of him. I know there is something wrong with my soul in its refusal to be comforted, but I am stuck on myself. I can't take my eyes off myself, and that is the cause of my greatest troubles. Our problem is not that outward troubles come, or even that we respond with strong emotions of unrest. The problem occurs when our condition begins to control us. Lesser problems grow greater with out-of-control thoughts and excessive introspection. We end up refusing to be comforted.

Asaph reflects on the physical symptoms of this condition. In verse 4 he says to the Lord, "You hold my eyelids open; I am so troubled that I cannot speak." We lay awake at night, with our overactive minds hard at work. We replay the problem over in our minds, hoping that maybe if we dwell on the situation long enough, a solution will come. At times, we are so troubled we can't even put words together to describe how we are doing. We don't have the energy to be around others or to engage in conversation.

The self-reflection continues in verses 5–6 with Asaph now thinking of better days in the past. "I consider the days of old, the years long ago. I said, 'Let me remember my song in the night.'" *Life used to be easier. I used to be a more joyful person. I had a closer relationship with God at that point in the past.* The comparison, however, doesn't prove fruitful.

Asaph fires off a series of questions in verses 7–9:

> "Will the Lord spurn forever, and never again
> be favorable?
> Has his steadfast love forever ceased?
> Are his promises at an end for all time?
> Has God forgotten to be gracious?
> Has he in anger shut up his compassion?"

This is what it's like to be in Doubting Castle. It's not so much that we doubt the existence of God as it is that we doubt his goodness—his care for us. *Why isn't God helping me out of this? Doesn't he see that I'm in over my head? Why is God doing this to me? Doesn't he care about me? Isn't he loving and gracious toward me?*

Dealing with the Darkness

What should we do in these moments of discouragement, doubt, and despair? How should we respond when thoughts of God don't seem to help, our soul refuses to be comforted, and we feel stuck in ourselves? We are fighting for faith, but our hearts are heavy, and our focus is distracted.

Even when thoughts of God don't seem to make a difference, the starting point is to remember what we know to be true, regardless of how it affects us. Remember the tenderness and the power of Christ. Know that his compassion for you remains strong, even when you do not perceive it. He will not forget us even when we have forgotten him. His hold on us remains even when our hold on him fails. Isaiah 50:4 speaks of one who knows "how to sustain with a word him who is weary." This is Christ. Two verses later it says, "I gave my back to those who strike, and my cheeks to those who pull out the beard; I hid not my face from disgrace and spitting" (Isaiah 50:6).

Jesus faced distress at Calvary so that he might comfort us in all our distress. And now, he specializes in sustaining the weary and dealing tenderly with the weak. He is skillful and mighty in this work.

The Lord is tender and gentle with our souls, while we often handle ourselves harshly. When Satan accuses us and Giant Despair beats us, too often we join in and reproach ourselves. We speak to ourselves the way Job's friends spoke to him, as miserable comforters.

Try to avoid self-condemning thoughts in the dungeon. Don't instinctively beat yourself up if you are in the darkness of doubt and despair. If Christ promises he will not break a bruised reed, think twice before taking the reed of your soul and trying to snap it in half. If Christ promises he will not put out the smoldering wick of our faith, we should not look at the wick as if it is already extinguished.

In self-condemnation, we mentally exaggerate the extremity of our condition. We convince ourselves that we are miserable all the time, even if those who know us well are prepared to testify that we are often walking in faith and joy. We exaggerate the effect of our condition on others, while our children and friends continue to enjoy our company as much as ever. We feel that we are horrible people for having these doubts. We become preoccupied with our doubts. Rather than helping, this drives us even further into despair.

We also condemn ourselves and deal harshly with ourselves when we think that our troubles are unique, or when we look at our doubting souls as an automatic sign that we are walking in unbelief and sin. We must skillfully diagnose our condition, which is best done with the help of a trusted friend. Others who know us well will see more clearly than we see ourselves. Meet with a friend to share your thoughts and struggles. If appropriate, confess your sins. Tell them where you need help. Ask them to remind you of the truth of God's power and grace. Request an honest opinion of how you are doing.

Remember that we are complex creatures, and there are many causes of darkness and doubt. Maybe the cause is sin and spiritual neglect, but maybe not.

Os Guinness, in his book *God in the Dark*, insightfully warns against super-spirituality in diagnosing our own condition. He says that if you doubt because you are tired, the best remedy is not to pray but to sleep. If you are plagued with doubt because you are exhausted from overwork, what you might need is not spiritual heart-searching but a day off or a vacation or some time in the sun. If you are feeling down, it could be that what you most need is some exercise or a better diet or an evening watching Netflix with friends.[2]

A Change in Focus

We have seen in Psalm 77:1–9 that the psalmist is honest about his condition. This honesty is not a sin. It is useful to acknowledge our condition. Christ invites us to come to him with all our burdens and to tell him all about our troubles. He has not only carried our sins; he carries our sorrows. He speaks peace to us in the middle of the torment and fear.

As we are forthright with God, we become fixated on him rather than on our doubts. Once we have diagnosed the problem so far as we are able, we do not dwell on the problem excessively. There is little progress to be made in overcoming doubt and despair by overanalyzing our doubt and despair. The more we see our doubt, the more we are inclined to doubt. The more we see our despair, the more we despair at the sight of it. Focusing on our circumstances is never the ultimate solution to our struggles. In Psalm 25:15 David says, "My eyes are ever toward the LORD, for he will pluck my feet out of the net." His eyes are not set on the net; they are set on the Lord.

Because the darkness turns us inward, escaping the darkness requires a change in focus. This is the biblical process for escaping gloomy introspection. We fight doubt by feeding our faith. Christ rescues us by turning our thoughts away from ourselves.

Let's return now to Psalm 77. In verse 10, Asaph moves from honestly expressing his troubles, and focusing on those difficulties, to focusing on the Lord. He turns from despairing introspection to a faith-filled declaration of the character of God: "Then I said, 'I will appeal to this, to the years of the right hand of the Most High.'" It is not enough to stop thinking about ourselves. We must fill our minds with that which is praiseworthy.

What does Asaph remember, ponder, and meditate on? It is no longer his condition, his distress, nor his inclination to doubt and despair. His thoughts are now Godward: "I will remember the deeds of the LORD; yes, I will remember your wonders of old. I will ponder all your work, and meditate on your mighty deeds" (vv. 11–12).

Where will I set my mind? On the holiness and incomparability of God! "Your way, O God, is holy. What god is great like our God?" (v. 13). This God works on our behalf! "You with your arm redeemed your people" (v. 15). His redemption was mighty when he parted the Red Sea: "Your way was through the sea, your path through the great waters; yet your footprints were unseen" (v. 19).

When his people were surrounded by enemies, helpless and stuck with nowhere to go, the Lord displayed his greatness and his goodness, and in remembering this Asaph gains strength to face his own challenges. Asaph concludes with a calm expression of confidence in God's care: "You led your people like a flock by the hand of Moses and Aaron" (v. 20).

God has done all this and more by giving his only Son for us when we were surrounded by our enemies—sin and death and hell. Therefore, even when his footprints are unseen, we know his ways are good. In light of the cross, our perspective can change even when our circumstances do not.

When we face the darkness, we also must call to mind truths about God.

- What do you know to be true about the character of God and his posture toward you? Consider writing it down.
- How has God saved you in Christ? What does this reveal about his love and commitment to you?
- How have you experienced the Lord working on your behalf? Ask a friend to remind you of how God has sustained, provided for, and protected you in the past.

Praise God for a time he brought you through the darkness or empowered you to honor him during a trial.

The Promises of Christ

How did Christian and Hopeful escape Doubting Castle and Giant Despair? It was not until Christian realized that he had a key called Promise that opened all the doors and gates of Doubting Castle. Later, Giant Despair is beheaded and Doubting Castle is destroyed. This is to show that although our battle against despair is great and often wearying, we know the outcome is secure, and the downfall of doubt and despair is certain.

As the castle is destroyed, two good and honest people are saved and brought out of captivity alive: Mr. Despondency, who had almost starved to death, and his daughter Much-afraid. Soon, Much-afraid was dancing happily in her freedom, and Mr. Despondency ate some food to revive his spirits.

The day is coming when we too will dance and feast. "Weeping may tarry for the night, but joy comes with the morning" (Psalm 30:5).

The reason for our hope is that we have a key called Promise. And through the great and precious promises of God, he rescues us from the dungeon of despairing introspection. John Owen says, "The life and soul of all our comforts lie treasured up in the promises of Christ."[3] There are comforts here for you. If you are ensnared in introspective doubts and despair, turn now to the promises of God.

- Are you weak? "A bruised reed he will not break, and a faintly burning wick he will not quench" (Isaiah 42:3).
- Is your heart broken and downcast? "The LORD is near to the brokenhearted and saves the crushed in spirit" (Psalm 34:18).
- Does sin steal your joy? "If we confess our sins,

he is faithful and just to forgive us our sins and to cleanse us from all unrighteousness" (1 John 1:9).

- Are you suffering? "When you pass through the waters, I will be with you; and through the rivers, they shall not overwhelm you; when you walk through fire you shall not be burned, and the flame shall not consume you" (Isaiah 43:2).
- Do changing circumstances overwhelm you? "The eternal God is your dwelling place, and underneath are the everlasting arms" (Deuteronomy 33:27).
- Are you weary? "Come to me, all who labor and are heavy laden, and I will give you rest" (Matthew 11:28).
- Do you fear the future? "Surely goodness and mercy shall follow me all the days of my life" (Psalm 23:6).

Are you trapped in the dungeon today? Remember Asaph's example. Take your cares to the Lord in prayer. Know that the Good Shepherd is leading you, even when his footprints are unseen. Remember the unchanging goodness and power of God. Cling to the promises of Christ. Receive the comfort and strength of the indwelling Spirit. Refuse to wallow in your misery. Use the key and *run*.

And if despair still gets the upper hand, if we find that we cannot move outside ourselves, and the darkness does not lift, still we do not lose heart. Christ will one day come and perform the final rescue. And on that great day, Giant Despair will fall and Doubting Castle will be torn down forever.

Questions for Reflection and Discussion

- When you are stuck in introspection, what have you found most helpful?
- How do the words of Asaph in Psalm 77 help us when we are stuck on ourselves?

6
Fighting False Guilt

There is a type of guilt that leads to nothing good

Several years ago I was interacting with a friend in his mid-twenties who was troubled about his lifestyle and his future. He had grown up reading the stories of missionaries from centuries past who had left everything for the gospel. He had recently heard of Christians who had sold their homes and took other radical steps to avoid wealth.

My friend told me that he did not want to settle into an American lifestyle. He was uncomfortable with the prospect of living in a culture of consumerism. How can it be okay to have a kitchen stockpiled with food when so many in the world are starving? How could he possibly join a church with an expensive building and nice furniture when so many people in the world are homeless? When he reads the story of the rich young ruler in Luke 18, he feels guilty for being as rich as he is. He was considering leaving the country because he did not see how living in America could be compatible with the call to sacrificial discipleship. At points, he spoke through tears.

More recently, I met a woman after Sunday service. It was her first Sunday at the church. As she was telling me her story, she mentioned that she was a recently divorced single parent. She hung her head as she spoke. I told her I was sorry. I mentioned that we have a number of divorced people in the church, and told her I have a lot of respect for single parents. I said I hoped she felt at home here, and expressed confidence that she would be welcomed and loved by the people of the church. Her eyes lit up, as if surprised she hadn't received the rejection she was expecting, and then she cried.

Guilt is a burden that many believers carry every day. It is the soundtrack in our minds, the white noise relentlessly hissing in our ears. Persistent guilt afflicts the insecure and the confident alike.

Where do you experience a sense of guilt and failure? Do you keep a mental list of the ways you are failing? Do you live with a vague sense that you are doing a lot of things wrong? Do you feel guilty for not being a great friend? Do you feel guilty as a church member, guilty as a parent and spouse, guilty as a disciple of Christ?

The Lord does not intend for us to go through life this way. One of the ways Christ bears our burdens is by graciously exposing the presence of false guilt in our lives.

Not All Guilt Is Good

Feelings are a fallible guide to identifying guilt. We need to distinguish between *feeling* guilty and *being* guilty. There are some things in our lives that we should feel guilty about, but we don't. At the same time, there are things we feel guilty about, but we shouldn't. The first category is one Christians are usually familiar with—real guilt in our lives that we are unaware of or unaffected by. In these instances, we ask God to search us for hidden faults, convict us of sin, and lead us once again to Christ to experience the riches of forgiveness.

But the second category doesn't receive as much attention. Here, we are deeply aware of and affected by a sense of guilt, but it is a false guilt. We are not in the wrong before God in the ways we think we are. It is possible—and in fact, common among Christians—to feel guilty about areas of our lives that God is pleased with. We bear false witness against ourselves.

False guilt preys on the weak, but it is not humility. It is a form of self-preoccupation. David Prince, in his article "The Accuser in the Mirror," says, "Wallowing in false guilt is the fruit of fixing one's gaze on oneself rather than on the acceptance and freedom found in the gospel of Jesus Christ."[1] This false or misplaced guilt gains its power by disguising itself as true guilt. The moment we see that type of guilt as unfounded before God, it loses its ability to discourage us.

Even in our misplaced guilt, God is gracious to us. We are not without hope. Guilt will not have the last word. Jesus Christ rescues us from all guilt, both real and imagined. He forgives us of true guilt, and he frees us from false guilt. In doing so, he restores to us the joy of his salvation.

The Air We Breathe

We live in a world of guilt. Sometimes the guilt we feel is over spiritual matters. We hear that someone keeps a journal, and we feel guilty for not keeping one. A friend says he went on a thirty-minute prayer walk, and we feel guilty that we haven't done the same. Everyone is talking about a Christian book that has revolutionized their spiritual life; but when you read it, you find the language is too archaic or the approach too philosophical. You think something is wrong with you because you are not benefiting from the book.

We also feel guilty about the things we enjoy in life: the food we eat, the cars we own, the home we live in, the amount of clothes we have, the frivolous things we buy, the ways we use our time. Our Father in heaven delights to give us good things to enjoy, but we constantly second-guess our experience of his generosity. Where he is lavish toward us, we are stingy and overly scrupulous. Where he gives no laws, we make laws for ourselves. We feel guilty about our failure to exercise ("I'm so lazy"), and then we feel guilty about giving so much time to exercise ("I'm so vain"). We feel guilty about overworking, and then we feel guilty when we rest because we know there is always more to be done.

The genuine guilt of conviction of sin is a work of the Holy Spirit. But we can make people feel guilty on our own, without the Spirit's help. Leaders are aware of the power of guilt to incite people to action. If you can make people feel guilty, you get results. If people haven't learned the skill of distinguishing between real and false guilt, they will never know the difference. In the case of false guilt, the results rarely last, but the immediate response people have—the sorrow and the perception of a need for personal change—give false guilt its appeal.

The Comparison Trap

In any area of life, differences with others contribute to our experience of guilt: our diverse temperaments, circumstances, gifts, and convictions. False guilt thrives on unhealthy comparisons with others. A mother feels guilty for not naturally displaying a lot of physical affection toward her kids. A businessperson feels guilty because a coworker is a lot better at managing email. A husband feels guilty because he is not handy around the house. A teenager feels guilty because he doesn't have the same people skills as his peers. A highly emotional person wishes she was calmer and more levelheaded; a less emotional person wishes she wasn't so stoic and unaffected by life.

Parenting is a minefield for false guilt and unhealthy comparisons. Suppose a mother posts a picture on Instagram of their family camping trip. In the photo, the morning sun is rising, and Dad is doing family devotions while the kids are preparing and cooking the fish they caught that morning. The comment accompanying the photo says, "Our annual two-week camping trip is always the highlight of our year! So grateful for the extended break, the laughter and memories, the time outdoors away from technology, and the opportunity for our kids to experience the joys of simple living." A cluster of hashtags follows: "#GreatFamilyDevotions #MakingMemories #PureJoy."

You see this post, and you tank. *We are not consistent enough with family devotions. We don't enjoy each other the way other families do. I am not giving my children enough meaningful childhood experiences, and it is going to hinder their development. My kids spend too much time looking at screens, and it's ruining their lives.* Many parents find it difficult to labor in faith and joy because of the persistent presence of guilt.

When an introspective person spends time with someone who expresses opinions in an overconfident and dogmatic manner, it is common for the introspective person to feel judged. We have negative thoughts of ourselves, and simultaneously become defensive toward others. Introspective people who are frail and have sensitive consciences are more inclined to respond to perceived judgments with negative thoughts of themselves ("I'm a failure for never taking my kids camping"). Introspective people who are confident and self-assertive will be more inclined to defend themselves from perceived judgment by judging in return ("She thinks she's so much better than everyone because her family goes camping"). The only way we know to escape feelings of inferiority is to try to view ourselves as superior to everyone else.

Sometimes false guilt is the fruit of envy. *I want to be good like that. I want to be popular like that.* We don't rest in being God's children, and we are hungry for more assurances of our worth. Therefore, in the process of turning from false guilt, we often need to repent of other real sins, such as envy, pride, and selfishness.

Essential Distinctions for Fighting False Guilt

Distinction #1: Divine vs. Human Approval

False guilt has a strong horizontal element: What are others thinking of me? Do they approve of me? Am I failing or disappointing others? The fear of man is a snare (Proverbs 29:25). One way the fear of man ensnares us is by weighing us down with the false guilt that comes from seeking the approval of others. People are ready to issue judgments on us for any number of things. But our Father does not want us to be controlled by human opinions or enslaved to cultural expectations. We must learn to be content with others thinking less of us. And we must learn to distinguish between the assessments of others and the assessments of our Father in heaven.

The gospel compels us to live for Christ and overthrows people-pleasing and self-approval. In Galatians 1:10 Paul says, "For am I now seeking the approval of man, or of God? Or am I trying to please man? If I were still trying to please man, I would not be a servant of

Christ." In 1 Corinthians 4:3, he adds, "But with me it is a very small thing that I should be judged by you or any human court." His outlook on life doesn't rise and fall with the encouragement or criticism of others because the perspective of others is "a very small thing." In the next verses, he says, "It is the Lord who judges me," and when Christ returns, "each one will receive his commendation from God" (1 Corinthians 4:4–5).

We spend so much of our time and energy making negative judgments, condemning ourselves, and condemning each other. But when Christ comes, human *condemnation* gives way to divine *commendation*, and all those who are in Christ will receive personal affirmation from the King. Therefore, not only is God's assessment of us more important than all other assessments, it is often far more gracious.

Distinction #2: Accurate vs. Inaccurate Self-Assessments

Learn to distrust your evaluation of yourself. Self-evaluations are unreliable and often inaccurate. We are capable of thinking of ourselves more positively than we ought, and we are capable of thinking of ourselves more negatively than we ought. Don't make the mistake of investing every negative self-assessment with divine authority. Our guilty self-assessments must be submitted to Scripture.

God's Word reveals God's perspective of his children and exposes the presence of false guilt. When you feel guilty because you don't think you have any useful spiritual gifts, or because you think your life isn't making any difference in the lives of others, remember that God says "each has received a gift" (1 Peter 4:10). It is likely he is using you in ways you are unaware. When you feel guilty because you think you are no longer growing as a Christian, and it seems you are only becoming more anxious or irritable or angry, remember that God is at work in you, both to will and to work for his good pleasure (Philippians 2:13). When you feel guilty because you have been physically or emotionally abused, and you think it's your fault that someone verbally battered you or sexually violated you, remember that victimization is real, and each person is responsible for his or her own sin (Deuteronomy 24:16). It's not your fault.

Negative self-assessments assail us: *I am not a good friend to others. I am failing as a spouse. My prayer life is nonexistent.* Of course, it is possible that a negative self-assessment is accurate. But it's also possible that we perceive failure, wrongdoing, or sin in our lives where it does not exist. Such assessments are often emotionally driven, reactionary, and they have not been confirmed by others. A trusted friend or two can help us sort through our negative thoughts about ourselves and guide us in determining their accuracy.

Distinction #3: Weakness vs. Sin

Lou Priolo provides three categories of inferiority judgments, or negative assessments, of ourselves:

1. Inaccurate perception

2. Accurate but not sinful

3. Accurate and sinful.[2]

This general categorization is useful in the fight against false guilt. Not only must we distinguish between inaccurate and accurate perception, but we must also realize that accurate perceptions are not necessarily sinful.

I don't think I am good with directions, and that is accurate. I don't think I am a good singer, and that is also quite accurate and has been confirmed by many. When I get allergy attacks, I feel weak and useless, and it's true. But these things are not sinful, and we shouldn't feel guilty over weaknesses.

John Newton says it is common for Christians to "overcharge ourselves." Not that we think we are worse than we really are, but that we charge ourselves with guilt over weaknesses and impediments that are not sinful. He mentions, as examples, a poor memory and a distressed spirit. We needlessly burden and oppress ourselves, Newton says, by charging ourselves with guilt where there is only weakness and no sin.[3]

Sin is to be repented of, while weaknesses and limitations are to be boasted in.

Therefore I will boast all the more gladly of my weaknesses, so that the power of Christ may rest upon me. For the sake of Christ, then, I am content with weaknesses, insults, hardships, persecutions, and calamities. For when

I am weak, then I am strong. (2 Corinthians 12:9–10)

Distinction #4: Temptation vs. Sin

We often feel guilty for being tempted, even when we don't give in to temptation. But temptation is not a sin. Jesus was tempted in every way, as we are, yet without sin (Hebrews 4:15). Don't beat yourself up because you are strongly tempted. When you resist temptation, God is pleased, and you are not guilty.

Distinction #5: Responsibility vs. Concern

There's an idea I first encountered through author Paul Tripp that helps distinguish between responsibility and concern.[4] Imagine drawing a circle on a page—it's called a circle of responsibility. Everything within this circle of responsibility represents what God has called us to do. Then imagine drawing a larger concentric circle around the smaller circle. This larger circle is the circle of concern, representing things that concern me but are beyond my ability, and therefore are not my responsibility.

This matters because we often think that everything that concerns us is our responsibility. We pull all our cares into the smaller circle, which produces guilt.

- Parents who are faithfully raising their child feel guilty because he is a living terror and daily throws temper tantrums.
- A man shares the gospel with his friends and

family but feels guilty because he has not led any of them to Christ.

- A single woman feels guilty for not being married.
- An elderly man feels guilty because his grown daughter has turned her back on God.

In each of these cases, there is a failure to distinguish between responsibility and concern. While sorrow may be an appropriate response, guilt is not. In fact, each person has fulfilled his or her responsibility to God; the results themselves are in God's hands.

Distinction #6: Principle vs. Practice

There is a difference between biblical principles that must be obeyed and specific practices or methods that are one of many potential applications of a biblical principle. A *principle* is a basic truth that guides our actions; a practice is a specific way of doing something.

For example, a principle is to treasure God's Word; a practice is to have a plan to read through the Bible in a year. A principle is to disciple your children; a practice is to schedule weekly one-on-one time with each of your kids. A principle is to love your wife; a practice is to write her a poem.

Practices that flow from biblical principles are commendable. In fact, practices are essential if we are to faithfully apply God's Word. But specific practices are not to be confused with biblically mandated principles. Otherwise, we will think we are failing to obey a divine command simply because we are not implementing a particular practice. Success or godliness in a particular area—whether it's personal devotions, church life, parenting, marriage, or education—soon becomes equated with a particular way of doing things.

Are You Truly Guilty?

The path of false guilt never leads to joy in Christ because it is a path paved with self-preoccupation and self-deception. When we confess false guilt, we often go on feeling guilty. This is because we are failing to properly diagnose the problem. By God's grace, we can learn over time not to feel guilty unless we truly are guilty according to Scripture.

But what if our guilt is real? What if we discover that our negative thoughts of ourselves are accurate and reveal the presence of iniquity in the sight of God? And for that matter, what if even our false guilt is grounded in envy, jealousy, and selfishness?

Praise God, we have a Savior, and he has taught us what to do. We repent. We confess our sins and run to Christ just as we did the day we first believed. "I acknowledged my sin to you, and I did not cover my iniquity; I said, 'I will confess my transgressions to the LORD,' and you forgave the iniquity of my sin" (Psalm 32:5). True repentance and confession lead to rejoicing, as Christ removes the burden of guilt. "Whoever conceals his transgressions will not prosper, but he who confesses and forsakes them will obtain mercy" (Proverbs 28:13). "In him we have redemption through his blood, the forgiveness of our trespasses, according to the riches of his grace" (Ephesians 1:7).

We cast the burdens of real guilt and false guilt upon the Lord. And we rest our guilty souls in the joy of knowing that "There is therefore now no condemnation for those who are in Christ Jesus" (Romans 8:1).

Questions for Reflection and Discussion

- What does false guilt look like in your life?
- Which distinction in this chapter is most helpful to you in fighting false guilt?

7
Rescuing Self-Reflection

How to examine our lives without losing our sanity

The solution to excessive self-reflection and unhelpful introspection is not casting off all self-examination. Instead, we look to Christ and learn how to examine ourselves in a way that strengthens our faith in him and deepens our joy in him.

How can we evaluate ourselves the way God intends? How do we examine ourselves without losing our sanity? How do we exchange the aimless, renegade self-reflection that often accompanies introspection for purposeful self-reflection that leads to edification and honors God?

It's time to consider the dangerous but essential duty of self-examination.

Self-Evaluation at 11 P.M.

Nancy Wilson shares a scenario under the heading "Self-Evaluation at 11 P.M." She is writing to mothers, but there is application for everyone. Consider the following:

It's been a long day. You were up at 5:30 with the baby, got a good breakfast on the table for husband and kids. Got the lunches packed, the kids off to school, cleaned up, showered, dressed, fed the baby again, read to the toddler(s), got the six-year-old working on his letters and the eight-year-old working on math, stopped for lunch, put the little ones down for naps, baked cookies, folded clothes, watered the petunias, took the kids to the park, listened to the events of the school day over cookies and milk, fixed dinner, greeted your husband, served dinner, cleaned up, gave four baths, read bedtime stories, snuggled with the little ones, fixed your husband some coffee, and collapsed in a chair to enjoy it with him. After an hour of visiting or reading you can't keep your eyes open. You look at the pile of ironing that didn't get done, and you remember the letter you meant to write, but sigh and go to bed.

Suddenly you are wide awake. Now with a quiet moment to think, thoughts flood into your mind. You remember that on top of the unfinished ironing you were short with your daughter when she asked for the third time when dinner would be ready. You confess it to God, but you still feel bad.

You wish you had spent more time coloring with your six-year-old. You remember his look of disappointment when you told him you had to hang out the laundry. Now your stomach is in a knot. What a terrible mother you are, you tell yourself. You don't even act like a Christian. You didn't even read your Bible today, and you haven't for three days. Besides, you've gained five pounds and you look terrible. No self-discipline at all. And if you were really disciplined, you would work out. Your husband is probably unhappy about those five pounds, you tell yourself. And so it goes on.[1]

God Is Not the Author of Accusation

The details don't fit us all, but the tendency toward what I'll call "renegade self-reflection" resonates with many of us. The quiet moment in which evaluative thoughts flood our minds could come to the man who is driving home from work or the teenager on the bus after school, or the college student who just finished a difficult semester, or the pastor on a Sunday afternoon.

We often engage in self-evaluation when our discouragement and unruly emotions drive us there. We are low on sleep, we are worn down by responsibilities and busyness, and we apparently think that is the perfect time to solve all the problems of our souls.

In our above example, Wilson goes on to explain that most of us are not going to do our best self-evaluation after 10:30 p.m., at the end of a tiring day. Introspection is not likely to be fruitful if we take that approach, and more often than not it will only produce anxiety, depression, and self-condemning thoughts. She reminds us, "God is not the author of accusation and condemnation of His children. He chastises and forgives, He delights to show mercy. He is the Father of all comfort. He does not pile on accusations in the night!"[2]

Some Practical Suggestions

God intends for self-evaluation to be fuel—not buckets of water—thrown on the fires of our faith. How can we avoid having our self-examination hijacked by unhealthy introspection? How can we examine ourselves without losing sight of God?

Start with Christ.

Self-evaluation will never be helpful if we are in a self-centered frame of mind. Our sinful self-absorption quickly turns self-evaluation into morbid introspection, robbing us of joy and faith. Charles Spurgeon says, "Any practice that detracts from faith is an evil practice, but especially that kind of self-examination which would take us away from the cross-foot, proceeds in a wrong direction."[3]

This is why we must always look upward before looking inward. Only when we are consciously dwelling in the shadow of the cross are we able to examine ourselves with humility and faith. At the cross, I see the Son of God who loved me and gave himself for me. Because of his death for sinners, I am forgiven and loved by one who knows me fully. There is no sin or weakness in me that takes God off guard. He knows far more of my sin than I do, yet he loves me still and his goodness and mercy will follow me all the days of my life (Psalm 23:6). In Christ I have the promise that he who began a good work in me will bring it to completion (Philippians 1:6).

Have a purposeful approach.

Self-evaluation needs to be contained. It should be periodic, not constant. It should not be the result of a wandering mind, but should be approached with purpose. Some decisions or areas of life you may want to evaluate on a monthly or annual basis. The best way to evaluate the health and progress of a tree is not by examining it every day. A minute of purposeful, faith-filled reflection on our hearts and lives will do more good than an hour of aimless, fretting self-reflection.

Choose the right time.

Remember that the more fragile your condition, the less accurate and fruitful your assessments will be. If you are tired, wait until you are rested. If you are in a discouraged or exhausted frame of mind, hit the eject button and abandon self-assessment until a later time. Always ask the question, is this a good time for self-evaluation?

Self-evaluation should happen off the playing field. We need to be able to see all of the players from further back. This is what coaches do. Players do it also, not so much during the game but when they review video afterward. Players will be more absorbed in the activity while the clock is running. They can't see the big picture involving all the players.

This is why an evening to yourself, or a daylong personal retreat, or a few prayerful minutes in the quiet of the morning, will produce more fruitful self-reflection than all of the unfruitful self-reflective thoughts that come at us throughout the day.

Ask for God's help.

We want to respond to the Holy Spirit, not self-accusations. The issue is not what we think of ourselves, but what God thinks of us. Therefore, we pray for the Spirit to search us, and ask God to show us our hearts. Join the psalmist in praying, "Search me, O God, and know my heart! Try me and know my thoughts! And see if there be any grievous way in me, and lead me in the way everlasting!" (Psalm 139:23–24).

Base your evaluations on the Bible.

Our self-assessments are often based on unhelpful comparisons with others or centered on things that are not most important. We should focus our evaluation on biblical categories such as character and example, faithfulness to God in the roles he has given us, and stewardship of the resources he has entrusted to us.

Look for grace.

We not only look at ourselves to see where we need to grow; we look at ourselves to see where we have grown. By the grace of God, we are not what we once were. We should go through life with an awareness of the ways God is at work in us. At the end of the day or week or year, examine yourself not only to see where the forgiving grace of God is needed, but also to see where the empowering and transforming grace of God is at work. In which areas of my life is God pleased with me? Which areas am I walking in obedience to him? How is he using me in the lives of others?

I am convinced most Christians are unpracticed in identifying and thanking God for the good that he has placed in their hearts and lives. The next chapter will further examine this neglected theme.

Keep it short.

Self-assessment doesn't take a long time. Avoid aimlessly hunting for sin and endlessly turning things over in your mind. Be aware that when you look inward, your heart and mind and will are no longer engaging in their normal activity. C. S. Lewis explains how self-reflection can backfire.

> In introspection we try to look "inside ourselves" and see what is going on. But nearly everything that was going on a moment before is stopped by the very act of our turning to look at it. Unfortunately this does not mean that

introspection finds nothing. On the contrary, it finds precisely what is left behind by the suspension of all our normal activities.[4]

Involve others.

We know ourselves most accurately through community. Make sure you are a member of a local church. Share your self-assessments with others and invite the input of others to see if they agree. It is not uncommon for us to have areas of our lives that we never learn to evaluate accurately on our own. Remember that "Where there is no guidance, a people falls, but in an abundance of counselors there is safety" (Proverbs 11:14). Have friends who are willing to speak the truth in love and to exhort you so that you will not be self-deceived (Hebrews 3:13).

Confess your sins.

I have sometimes asked my kids a few questions as they go to bed. One of those questions is, "What is one thing you did or didn't do today that reminded you of your need for a Savior?" If we are assessing ourselves honestly, we will see the sin that clings closely because we all stumble in many ways. Self-examination leads to confession of sin, and confession should always lead to greater joy in Jesus. The reason we momentarily look inward is so we can look to Christ and find mercy. "If we confess our sins, he is faithful and just to forgive us our sins and to cleanse us from all unrighteousness" (1 John 1:9).

Focus your application.

If there is an area of your life in which you are convinced God is calling you to grow and change, clarify what you believe God is calling you to in that area. What does faithfulness look like? Then, take a specific step of application. If you are convicted of prayerlessness, take time at that moment to pray. If you are convicted that you haven't been cherishing your wife, plan time with her or write a note for her. If you are convicted that you haven't been faithful in outreach, consider which neighbor you can invite over for dinner next month.

Discouragement and condemnation thrive on generalities and inaction. Spirit-empowered obedience chokes discouragement and proves our repentance. Set simple and attainable goals in the area God is calling you to change. Avoid a mind-set that says everything must change; that is rarely from the Spirit.

Resist Self-Pity and Discouragement

The litmus test of our self-examination is the answer to this question: *What does it produce in us?* Does it produce greater trust in Christ, greater joy and humility? Or, does it produce self-pity and discouragement? You will know healthy self-examination by its fruits.

If it leads to discouragement, it is not healthy self-examination. We need to be able to distinguish between biblical self-examination and unhealthy introspection in our lives. J. I. Packer is helpful in explaining the difference.

Whereas introspection, whether it ends in euphoria or in the gloom of self-pity and self-despair, can become an expression of self-absorbed pride, self-examination is the fruit of God-centered humility, ever seeking to shake free of all that displeases the Father, dishonors the Son and grieves the Holy Spirit, so as to honor God more. Thus self-examination is a fundamentally healthy process, leading into repentance, where mere introspection can leave us just feeling sorry for ourselves.[5]

The Puritan William Bridge, in his book *A Lifting Up for the Downcast*, has an insightful treatment of discouragement. He says that we tend to think our discouragement is a sign of humility. When I am discouraged, I am aware of my sin, my weakness, my ineffectiveness, and I feel terrible about it. That seems pretty humble. But in reality, discouragement is a hindrance to humility. It is a form of self-centeredness, because when I am discouraged I am more concerned about what my situation means for me than I am about my sin against God and the glory of God in my life.

True humility stubbornly refuses to wallow in self-absorbed misery. The more humbled we are about our sin, the less discouraged we will be about our sin. Humility always leads to comfort in Christ; discouragement leaves us in our misery. Bridge says that the more we are humbled by our sin, the more we will be found rejoicing in the Lord and strengthened in our duties. But the more we are discouraged, the less we rejoice in the Lord, and the more we are weakened for duty.[6]

Jesus rescues us from destructive self-examination, empowering us to examine our lives without losing our souls. Because of Christ, self-examination can lead to rejoicing in him, no matter what we find in ourselves. Be strengthened for all that God has called you to by the grace that is in Christ Jesus. Cast off self-pity and self-despair. Examine yourself. Fight the good fight with joy and faith, knowing that no matter how sinful or weak or flawed we may be, Christ our Captain is with us.

Questions for Reflection and Discussion

- Why is self-examination an important part of the Christian life?
- What is the difference between humility and discouragement as responses to self-examination?

8

Grace in the Mirror

Why we should see and celebrate the good in ourselves

When I assess myself regarding one of my roles, whether as a disciple, father, husband, friend, or pastor, my natural impulse is often to see nothing good. Take preaching, for example. If I am preparing a sermon, or reflecting on a sermon I've preached, it often seems that everything about the sermon is awful. On Saturdays, all the weaknesses of the sermon force themselves into my mind. All of the illustrations are bad. The exegesis is underdeveloped. There is not enough of Christ in the sermon. I am not giving people a big view of God. My application is too general. The introduction is boring. And on and on.

This kind of negative self-assessment is common among those who are overly introspective—not only before serving but afterward as well. I've learned that it's best for me to avoid self-evaluation of my sermons on Sunday afternoons. Evaluation must come, but it can happen later, with the help of others.

Something else I've noticed is that if I receive a lot of encouragement and one criticism in some area of life, it's the critique that lodges itself in my mind. That's my tendency with the annual job review I receive as an employee. The evaluation often contains encouragements, identifying and celebrating strengths and accomplishments. But the evaluation also includes areas where growth is needed. Inevitably, the encouragements ricochet off my soul while the constructive feedback cuts deep. I dwell on critiques and view them as defining my work.

None of this is humility. It is the pride of self-pity that wants to impress others so badly that I can't stop thinking about myself. But there is a way forward. It has to do with seeing grace in ourselves.

"That Was Pathetic"

Not long ago we had a guest preacher named Rick at church on a Sunday morning. As soon as he was done preaching, he returned to his seat beside me, gave me a beaming smile, and said, "That was fun!" Now, I do enjoy preaching, and I love my job. But of all the thoughts I tend to have immediately after preaching, *That was fun!* is not among the more common ones. I am far more likely to return to my seat after a sermon thinking, *That was pathetic.*

Is that the attitude we should have in our service? Here's what I've realized: "That was fun!" revealed a man focused on Christ and the joyful privilege of proclaiming the good news. In my case "That was pathetic" usually reveals a man focused on self and the assessment of others.

Are you aware of this tendency in your life? You are asked to share your testimony with a small group and you can't stop thinking about what a poor job you did. You are asked to use your musical gifts on a Sunday morning, and you are mostly aware of imperfections and mistakes. You approach a friend because you want to encourage her, but you walk away feeling like everything you said was incoherent and stupid. You try to share the gospel with someone, and nothing comes out right. You want to be faithful as a spouse or a parent, but it seems as though you are doing everything wrong. You walk away from most acts of service with the same thought: *That was pathetic.* It's there in our service, in our good works, in our obedience.

Seeing the good that God is doing in us and through us is an overlooked aspect of the Christian life. By his grace Christ is powerfully changing us and working through us. His gifts and graces adorn the lives of each of his children. That includes you. But too often, our view of ourselves excludes the good.

Richard Sibbes says that we need to "know our own graces." He explains, "A Christian should not only examine his heart for the evil that is in him, to be humbled; but [also examine his heart for] what good there is, that he may joy and be thankful."[1] This examination of our hearts and lives for what is good, followed by joyful thanksgiving to God, is one of the ways we resist morbid introspection. We must learn to see grace in the mirror.

Daily Moments of Divine Pleasure

Some of us are better at evaluating our lives than we are at enjoying the favor of God on our lives. We replay all our weaknesses and mistakes. We dwell on paralyzing comparisons. We are condemned over mixed motives. Deep down we think *That was pathetic* because we suspect God looks at our service and thinks the same.

Wayne Grudem says, "I suspect that just as Satan accuses Christians and wants them to feel false guilt and false accusation, so he also seeks to keep them from the great joy of knowing the favor of God on their daily activities, of knowing that God is pleased with their obedience."[2] That is one of the strategies of Satan in your life—keeping you from knowing the many moments of divine pleasure that shower you every day. He keeps us from feeling the love God has for us. Here is the truth, to be shouted from the rooftops:

> The LORD your God is in your midst,
> a mighty one who will save;
> he will rejoice over you with gladness;
> he will quiet you by his love;
> he will exult over you with loud singing.
> (Zephaniah 3:17)

Do you hear his singing over you? Are you aware of the favor of God on your daily activities? Do you know God is pleased with your obedience?

From the time our alarm clock goes off to the moment we rest our heads on our pillows at night, every day is packed with moments of divine pleasure for the children of God. Our Father wants us to go through our daily activities with a tangible sense of his pleasure in our obedience and service.

- Do you believe that God exists and that he rewards those who seek him? Hebrews 11:6 says this is faith that is pleasing to God.
- Have you shared with others or made sacrifices for others today? Hebrews 13:16 says, "Do not neglect to do good and to share what you have, for such sacrifices are pleasing to God."
- Are there any ways you are resisting being conformed to this world? Romans 12:1–2 says this is acceptable or pleasing in God's sight.
- Do you ever pray for others? And are there ways you lead a peaceful and godly life? First Timothy 2:3 says, "This is good, and it is pleasing in the sight of God our Savior."
- Do you give financially? Philippians 4:18 says it is "a fragrant offering, a sacrifice acceptable and pleasing to God."
- Do you care for those in your home or support family members? First Timothy 5:4 says, "this is pleasing in the sight of God."

For every look to ourselves, take ten looks to Christ. And an important part of that one look to yourself is identifying the ways that your life is pleasing to God. We overlook that our Father is truly pleased with us when we obey.

This does not mean that our lives are perfectly pleasing to God in every way. Jesus is the only one who can say, "I always do the things that are pleasing to [the Father]" (John 8:29). It's true that God is displeased with us when we pursue sin, as any good Father would be. But this doesn't mean what we often think it means regarding God's daily posture toward us. Too often we live with a constant sense of God's displeasure.

As Christians, we walk in faith, obedience, and love for Christ. Therefore, our lives are fundamentally pleasing to God. Our Father does not intend for his children to go through life feeling like spiritual losers any more than a parent wants his or her kids to feel like losers. God rejoices over us, and he wants us to rejoice in his ongoing activity in our lives.

Does your growth seem slow? Does your obedience seem small and irrelevant? Learn to celebrate even the smallest acts of obedience. Treasure the tiniest evidences of the Spirit's work in you. John Newton urges Christians to remember to be thankful for what we consider little in our souls. "A little grace, a spark of true love to God, a grain of living faith, though small as a mustard-seed, is worth a thousand worlds. . . . It becometh the Lord's people to be thankful; and to acknowledge his goodness in what we have received, is the surest and most pleasantest method of obtaining more."[3]

Examine Yourselves . . . to See Christ in You

In 2 Corinthians 13:5, we receive the command to examine ourselves. But the context is revealing. Paul had been under significant critique, and the call for the Christians in Corinth to examine themselves is part of Paul's self-defense. He tells them to examine themselves in order to see that Jesus Christ is in them and as proof that Paul has been faithful as a minister. "Examine yourselves, to see whether you are in the faith. Test yourselves. Or do you not realize this about yourselves, that Jesus Christ is in you?"

Paul's argument hinges on the assumption that this self-examination is an encouraging one, confirming the indwelling presence of the risen Christ. We are to examine ourselves *to see that Christ is in us.*

In his letters, Paul frequently makes statements with the goal of helping Christians see evidences of God's grace in their own lives. He wants them to see grace in the mirror.

- To the church in Rome he writes, "your obedience is known to all, so that I rejoice over you" (Romans 16:19).
- To the church in Colossae, he calls their attention to the faith, love, and hope in their lives: "We heard of your faith in Christ Jesus and of the love that you have for all the saints, because of the hope laid up for you in heaven" (Colossians 1:4–5).
- To the church in Philippi, Paul encourages them toward continued obedience with the phrase,

"Therefore, my beloved, as you have always obeyed . . ." (Philippians 2:12). He wants them to acknowledge their own constant obedience to God.

- To the church in Corinth, he wants them to be aware of the abundance of spiritual gifts in their lives: "In every way you were enriched in [Christ] in all speech and all knowledge . . . so that you are not lacking in any gift" (1 Corinthians 1:5, 7). Writing later, Paul wants them to know that they "excel in everything—in faith, in speech, in knowledge, in all earnestness, and in our love for you" (2 Corinthians 8:7).

- To the church in Thessalonica, Paul wants them to know that the word of God is "at work in you believers" (1 Thessalonians 2:13). They are walking in a way that is pleasing to God: "We ask and urge you in the Lord Jesus, that as you received from us how you ought to walk and to please God, just as you are doing, that you do so more and more" (1 Thessalonians 4:1). Regarding their love for others: "Now concerning brotherly love you have no need for anyone to write to you, for you yourselves have been taught by God to love one another, for that indeed is what you are doing to all the brothers throughout Macedonia" (1 Thessalonians 4:9–10).

Couldn't many of these same things, and more, be said about you? Christians ought to live in the confidence of knowing that God is pleased with us in Christ. The

Lord wants us to be aware of our obedience and celebrate it as evidence of his power at work in us.

John Calvin noted that in Scripture, "Saints quite often strengthen themselves and are comforted by remembering their own innocence and uprightness."[4] This is what we see throughout the book of Psalms, where we frequently read declarations of innocence. In the New Testament, Paul makes statements about himself that reveal an understanding of God's grace in his own life.

- "I have lived my life before God in all good conscience up to this day" (Acts 23:1).
- "I worked harder than any of them, though it was not I, but the grace of God that is with me" (1 Corinthians 15:10).
- "I thank him who has given me strength, Christ Jesus our Lord, because he judged me faithful, appointing me to his service" (1 Timothy 1:12).

The good in us points not to us but to Christ. These are not self-produced strengths, but gifts and fruits of the Spirit. We have no autonomous worth or dignity or good without reference to God. We have no gifts or strengths that do not come from him. All is of grace, and all glory goes to God for what he has created, given, and sustains. The wise man truly has wisdom, and the mighty truly has strength, but this is no warrant for boasting (Jeremiah 9:23–24). "What do you have that you did not receive?" (1 Corinthians 4:7). The goal of seeing the good in our lives is always to boast in the Lord alone.

Overlooked No More

In the face of temptation, we sometimes think the scope of our sin and failure in a particular area is greater than it really is. Or, when we are faithful, we often think that our goodness is less than it really is. But the eyes of faith are able to see the situation from God's perspective, and align our view of ourselves with the Father's view of us.

Do you believe that the Lord sees your efforts to please him and that he delights in your good works? Hebrews 6:10 says, "For God is not unjust so as to overlook your work and the love you have shown for his name in serving the saints, as you still do." Where you are working hard, your Father in heaven does not overlook it. Where you are choosing love, he sees and he delights.

When a child does something well, what does his father do? He swoops his son off the ground, embraces him, high-fives him, beams over him. Why would we think our heavenly Father would respond to our service any differently?

Jesus says to the church in Ephesus, and to other churches in Revelation 2 and 3, "I know your works." The works he has in view in Ephesus are their good works, including their toil, their patient endurance, their discernment, and their opposition of evil. "I know you are enduring patiently and bearing up for my name's sake, and you have not grown weary" (Revelation 2:3). Every Christian should be comforted that Jesus knows our works.

This is especially strengthening and uplifting for those who see no grace or beauty in anything they do. Take to heart these words from J. C. Ryle:

> You see no beauty in any action that you do. All seems imperfect, blemished, and defiled. You are often sick at heart of your own shortcomings. But now know, that Jesus can see some beauty in everything that you do from a conscientious desire to please him. His eye can discern excellence in the least thing which is a fruit of his own Spirit. He can pick out the grains of gold from amid the dross of your performances, and sift the wheat from amid the chaff in all your doings. Your endeavors to do good to others, however feeble, are written in his book of remembrance. He does not forget your work and labor or love, however little the world may regard it.[5]

This is the tender promise of God to us. He sees beauty in your works. He remembers.

It is not promised that our work and our love will be remembered and praised by others, including the saints. At times, people will overlook your service. Maybe you know what it's like to receive more criticism than encouragement. You get criticized in the home, in your marriage, at work, and even as you serve the church. The people around you seem to be more aware of your shortcomings than your sacrifices. Your service is overlooked,

taken for granted, disregarded. Yet, we have it as a promise from God that he will not overlook our good works.

We have a Savior who makes our flawed and imper-
fect obedience beautiful in the sight of God. The heart
of our Father is *for us* in Christ. The Holy Spirit is active
in our lives.

So, preach the sermon and say "That was fun!" Serve
Christ, knowing that you will hear him say, "Well done,
good and faithful servant." Raise your children and experience God's pleasure in all your labors. Love others
as Christ loved you, knowing that God delights to see
his love shine through you. Believe that your daily good
works are adorning the gospel.

And let's fall asleep tonight free of vague feelings
of ineffectiveness and discouraging self-assessments.
Instead we can know the Father's smile upon us in his
Son and the many ways his Spirit is at work in us. Let's
learn to see grace in the mirror.

Questions for Reflection and Discussion

- Why is it important for Christians to "know our
  own graces"?
- Which Scripture can help you when you can't see
  good in anything you do, or when you are unaware
  of the Father's pleasure over your life?

9

"Cheer Up, You're Worse Than You Think"

Confession of sin is the path to joy in Christ

Jesus was eating in the home of a Pharisee. A woman who was known by many as a great sinner was there as well. She brought ointment to Jesus and began weeping. Then she did the unthinkable: "She began to wet his feet with her tears and wiped them with the hair of her head and kissed his feet and anointed them with the ointment" (Luke 7:38).

It was a stunning display of thankfulness and love for the one who came to seek and save the lost. The Pharisees objected because this woman was such a terrible sinner. But Jesus tells a parable to teach his disciples that the greater our awareness of our many sins, the greater our love for Christ will be. This woman's devotion to Christ and delight in him were proof that "her sins, which are many, are forgiven" (Luke 7:47).

We can face our many sins because Christ is a mighty Savior.

Some years ago I went through a time where it seemed as if I was growing more and more proud. I sat down and made a list of the various ways pride was surfacing in my life. It included things like

- caring too much about being associated with and recognized by people I respected;
- often failing to ask for the advice and opinion of others on important issues;
- using opportunities to serve as opportunities to try to impress;
- quickly disagreeing with and challenging those who are wiser and more experienced than I am;
- becoming argumentative and defensive when corrected;
- preferring teaching to learning.

Initially, I was discouraged. But God used that knowledge and confession of sin to lead me into a deeper love for Christ. Some faithful friends helped me see that I wasn't growing more proud; rather, the Spirit of God was allowing me to see my pride and grieve over it in new ways. It was evidence that God was maturing me and humbling me by his grace. They helped me understand that the Spirit of God delights to give his people a deeper awareness of sin—not to discourage us, but to grant us a deeper gratitude for the glory of the salvation we have received.

Repentance leads to rejoicing. Seeing sin is a doorway to savoring Christ.

Losing Sight of Sin?

There are popular teachers today who don't talk about sin or use the word *sinner* to describe Christians. Some make a practical argument, saying that Christians already know what they are doing wrong and that talking about sin will only bring them down. Others make a biblical argument, teaching that the New Testament norm is not for Christians to go through life with an ongoing awareness of sin. Others don't go quite so far, but advocate for less introspection and self-examination by saying that we shouldn't give too much attention to our sin.

This teaching is nothing new. In the second half of the nineteenth century, the subject of Christians' sins was brought to the forefront of discussion among Christians. From 1850–1875, what is called "The Higher Life Movement" became popular. The Higher Life Movement with its teaching on the victorious life was a concerted effort to minimize the doctrine of sin in the Christian life. They taught that the normal Christian life is not one of continual dissatisfaction with ourselves or daily awareness of sin, but a life of joy and victory in Christ. They taught that we are not sinners but saints, and that if we want to grow as Christians, we should not be concerned with our sins but with our salvation and with the glories of Christ.

In the early 1900s, theologian B. B. Warfield immersed himself in the teaching of the Higher Life Movement and concluded that their teaching suffered a shallow treatment of the Scriptures. He saw the teaching as a threat to the gospel of grace and the glory of Christ. Warfield understood that God's Word gives a high profile to sin and repentance in the life of the Christian.

"We all stumble in many ways" (James 3:2). Christians are lured and enticed by their own desires (James 1:14) because we are sinners (James 4:8). We must be warned against "an evil, unbelieving heart" that would lead us "to fall away from the living God" (Hebrews 3:12). Sin clings so closely to the Christian (Hebrews 12:1). When disciples of Jesus pray, we regularly confess our sins and ask God to forgive our debts (Matthew 6:12).

The New Testament letters teem with imperatives, exhortations, and warnings, all of which imply sin and imperfection—especially the repeated commands to mortify, cleanse, repent, and put off. The authors include themselves in these exhortations, frequently using the second person "we" and "us." They view all of Scripture as useful for teaching, correction, reproof, and training in righteousness (2 Timothy 3:16). This correcting and reproving speak clearly to the reality of remaining sin.

The Only Path to Joy in Christ

Warfield knew there was something profoundly mistaken with the idea that we grow in holiness by treating sin lightly. Our problem is not that we have too great a sense of our sin—the issue is how we *view* our sin. How long do we dwell there? How does seeing our sin lead us to fresh views of the grace that is in Christ Jesus?

Horatius Bonar is right that "Complaints against self, which do not lead the complainer directly to the cross, are most dangerous."[1] Sights of our sin that lead us to the cross, however, will not bring misery.

Knowing and confessing our sin leads us to greater joy in Christ. The Puritans used to say that it is through the tears of repentance that we see most clearly the brightness and glories of the saving cross.[2] On this point Warfield is fantastic:

> The Reformers presented the Christian life as a life of continuous dissatisfaction with self and of continuous looking afresh to Christ as the ground of all our hope. The effort of [the Higher Life teachers] to present the Christian life rather as a life of complete satisfaction with self tends not only altogether to undermine the entire evangelical system, but to strike a direct blow at the peace and joy of the Christian which is [their] professed object to secure.[3]

In other words, by attempting to attain joy and peace through a means other than dissatisfaction with self, we forfeit the very joy and peace we are aiming for. Cultivating a sense of dissatisfaction with self is the only path to joy in Christ. Warfield continues,

> For the Christian's peace and joy are not and cannot be grounded in himself, but in Christ alone. He rejoices in the sufficiency of Christ's

saving work for him; his exaltation is in a salvation made his despite his unworthiness of it. This joy obtains its peculiarity precisely from the coexistence of dissatisfaction with self and satisfaction with Christ. The dissatisfaction with self does not mar it; it enhances it rather—because the more dissatisfaction we feel with ourselves the more the greatness of Christ's salvation is manifest to us, and the more our delight in it waxes. . . . The spirit of [true] Christianity . . . is an attitude of exultant joy. Only this joy has its ground not in ourselves but in our Savior. We are sinners and we know ourselves to be sinners, lost and helpless in ourselves. But we are saved sinners; and it is our salvation which gives the tone to our life, a tone of joy which swells in exact proportion to the sense we have our ill-desert; for it is he to whom much is forgiven who loves much, and who, loving, rejoices much."[4]

Review the Day Briefly

The more we grow in godliness, the more we become aware of our sin. Throughout Scripture, God's people often express a deep sense of their own sinfulness and unworthiness.

- Abraham said, "Behold, I have undertaken to speak to the Lord, I who am but dust and ashes" (Genesis 18:27).

- Jacob said, "I am not worthy of the least of all the deeds of steadfast love and all the faithfulness that you have shown to your servant" (Genesis 32:10).
- Job said, "I am of small account" (Job 40:4) and "I despise myself, and repent in dust and ashes" (Job 42:6).
- David said, "I know my transgressions, and my sin is ever before me" (Psalm 51:3).
- Isaiah said, "Woe is me! For I am lost" (Isaiah 6:5).
- Peter said, "I am a sinful man, O Lord" (Luke 5:8).
- The tax collector said, "God, be merciful to me, a sinner!" (Luke 18:13).
- Paul said, "I am the very least of all the saints" (Ephesians 3:8), and
- "Christ Jesus came into the world to save sinners, of whom I am the foremost" (1 Timothy 1:15).

It is common among saints in Scripture to loathe and abhor themselves when they see their sin. Not all self-loathing is sinful. The new covenant promise of Ezekiel 36 includes receiving a new heart and having God's spirit within us; being empowered to obey God and being delivered from uncleanness; and knowing the abundance of God's blessing and the removal of our disgrace. In addition, God's perspective on sin is imparted to us. "Then you will remember your evil ways, and your deeds that were not good, and you will loathe yourselves for your iniquities and your abominations" (36:31).

None of this means that we sit around wallowing in our sin or that we are preoccupied with our sin. But it does mean that as we stand secure in God's grace, confident in our identity in Christ and with the hope of heaven in our eyes, we should regularly examine our lives for sin. We should confess our iniquity and walk in repentance.

A biblical definition of sin includes not only sins of commission but sins of omission. It includes not only intentional sins but unintentional sins. This means that we are far more sinful than we know. Jack Miller used to say, "Cheer up; you're worse than you think" and follow it up with "but you are more loved by Jesus than you can imagine."

Jerry Bridges says that because he knows the gospel is only for sinners, he begins each day by acknowledging that despite being a saint, he still sins much every day.[5] We all do. This is why we must examine our lives, including our words, our actions, our thoughts, and our motives. We confess to God the sins we are aware of, and we confess there are many sins in our lives we are unaware of.

John Stott writes,

> We all know that too much introspection can be unhealthy, unhelpful and even damaging. But some is not only salutary, but necessary. Our Bible reading will often sober and abase us in this way. The word of God ruthlessly exposes our sin, selfishness, vanity and greed, and then challenges us to repent and to confess. . . . It is a healthy discipline each evening to review the day briefly and call to mind our failures. Not

to do so tends to make us slapdash about sin and encourages us to presume on God's mercy, whereas to make a habit of doing so humbles and shames us, and increases our longing for greater holiness. There is nothing morbid about the confession of sins, so long as we go on to give thanks for the forgiveness of sins. It is fine to look inwards, so long as it leads us immediately to look outwards and upwards again.[6]

Calling to mind our sin is a good thing. But when you think about your sin, be on guard against stalling there in introspection. As Stott says, *briefly* review the day, and then allow inward looks to lead you *immediately* to look outward and upward to Christ.

Dealing with Persistent Guilt

If you are preoccupied with a besetting sin, or discouraged by your sin, remember that you have a Great High Priest who is praying for you even now. If regret over past sin weighs you down, remember that the finished work of Christ ensures that mercy and grace are always available in your time of need. Views of our sinfulness are meant to deliver us to a grander view of mercy.

However, this is not always our experience. We can feel stuck in the shadows of our failures. Is there a way out of this enduring sense of guilt? Yes.

Remember his heart toward you and his prayers for you. Remember that the Lord has blotted out your transgressions and will not remember your sins (Isaiah 43:25). Remember that all of God's justice was satisfied at the cross (Romans 3:26). Though he was angry with you, his anger turned away and was spent on Christ, that he might comfort you (Isaiah 12:1). "Christ Jesus is the one who died—more than that, who was raised—who is at the right hand of God, who indeed is interceding for us" (Romans 8:34).

You have been adopted in Christ! You are accepted by God! You are held fast by the one who has promised he will never forsake his own. Allow these truths to move you from guilt to forgiveness, from sorrow to joy, and from the bondage of self-focus to the freedom of praise.

It is good to have our hearts broken by sin. But we cannot allow sin to break our hope in Christ. Where sin abounds, his grace abounds all the more (Romans 5:20). The boundless grace of God has conquered our sin, and our misery is no match for the mercy of our God and Savior.

Whenever we talk about sin as pastors, parents, or friends, we should do so ultimately as a means of stunning people with unmerited grace. Most often, our problem is not that we are aware of too much of our sin, but that we must become more skilled in applying grace. Charles Spurgeon did this well.

> You cannot sin so much as God can forgive. If it comes to a pitched battle between sin and grace, you shall not be so bad as God is good. I will prove it to you. You can only sin as a man,

but God can forgive as God. You sin as a finite creature, but the Lord forgives as the infinite Creator.[7]

This is amazing grace! However great your sin, God's grace is greater! He does not forgive in part; he has forgiven all your iniquities! Therefore, "Bless the Lord, O my soul, and forget not all his benefits, who forgives all your iniquity" (Psalm 103:2–3). "He does not deal with us according to our sins, nor repay us according to our iniquities. For as high as the heavens are above the earth, so great is his steadfast love toward those who fear him; as far as the east is from the west, so far does he remove our transgressions from us" (Psalm 103:10–12).

Look often to the righteousness of Christ and his finished work on the cross. And when you are tempted to despair, to wallow in sinful self-contempt, to fall under Satan's accusations, and to hold on to persistent guilt—cheer up! You are worse than you think, but more loved than you have ever imagined. And in this love, our souls find rest.

Questions for Reflection and Discussion

- What are some of the ways the Bible emphasizes the reality of sin in believers?
- Can you think of a time in your life when repentance and confession led to greater joy in Christ?

10
Self-Forgetfulness

How to overcome our constant self-consciousness

Helen Keller was born in 1880 in Tuscumbia, Alabama. She was blind and deaf from infancy, and was therefore well acquainted with darkness, silence, isolation, and self-awareness. She devoted twenty-five years of her life learning how to read, write, and speak, so that she could communicate with others.

Helen wrote her first book when she was in her twenties, with the help of some of her friends. *The Story of My Life* covers her childhood through her time in college. This is how she described the challenges she faced and the lessons she learned in the midst of overwhelming darkness and despair:

> Everything has its wonders, even darkness and silence, and I learn, whatever state I may be in, therein to be content. Sometimes, it is true, a sense of isolation enfolds me like a cold mist as I sit alone and wait at life's shut gate. Beyond

there is light, and music, and sweet companionship; but I may not enter. Fate, silent, pitiless, bars the way. Fain would I question his imperious decree, for my heart is still undisciplined and passionate; but my tongue will not utter the bitter, futile words that rise to my lips, and they fall back into my heart like unshed tears. Silence sits immense upon my soul. Then comes hope with a smile and whispers, "There is joy in self-forgetfulness." So I try to make the light in others' eyes my sun, the music in others' ears my symphony, the smile on others' lips my happiness.[1]

When silence sits immense upon the soul, this is what hope teaches us: *There is joy in self-forgetfulness.*

Though most of us don't know the unique challenges of being blind or deaf, we do know the darkness of isolation. We know what it is to feel like we are trapped in ourselves, unable to escape. We know the burden of introspection.

But that is not all we know. Christians know that hope has a name. He is Jesus, and in his name is freedom for our souls. For all who are in Christ, there is light beyond the darkness and laughter beyond the silence. Knowing Jesus pulls us out of ourselves and gives relief from the burden of introspection. *There is joy in self-forgetfulness.*

Blessed Rest and True Joy

I remember the first time I read a brilliant little book by Tim Keller called *The Freedom of Self-Forgetfulness: The Path to True Christian Joy*. I read it again a few days later, and then read it out loud to my wife a few days after that. It is one of the most personally helpful things I've read on introspection.

Keller's goal is to lead Christians to "the blessed rest that only self-forgetfulness brings."[2] He does not advocate total self-forgetfulness in the sense that we no longer evaluate ourselves or that we are unaware of the activity of the Spirit and the flesh in our lives.

The goal is not absolute self-forgetfulness, but situational self-forgetfulness. We control our thoughts about ourselves, rather than our thoughts about ourselves controlling us. We learn to break free from constant self-consciousness. In short, we are more mindful about Christ than we are about ourselves. Keller says, "True gospel-humility means I stop connecting every experience, every conversation, with myself. In fact, I stop thinking about myself."[3]

Keller's book takes its cue from 1 Corinthians 3:21–4:7. The church in Corinth was full of boasting and relational strife. The apostle Paul explains to the Corinthians that their problem is a lack of humility, and he pushes them to adjust the way they think about themselves.

Paul explains how his own view of himself had changed in light of the gospel. First, he is no longer consumed with what others are thinking of him. He writes, "But with me it is a very small thing that I should be judged by you or by any human court" (1 Corinthians 4:3). So often our minds are fixed on ourselves, bound by introspection because we have placed ourselves in the courtroom of human opinions. We want others to think highly of us. We want to be better than others. If people criticize us, we are deflated. If we make a mistake, we are embarrassed. If people are more successful than us, we are ruined. But Paul says all of this is "a very small thing," because he refuses to be judged by any human court.

But then Paul goes one step further, and we must as well. "In fact, I do not even judge myself. For I am not aware of anything against myself, but I am not thereby acquitted" (1 Corinthians 4:3–4). Keller explains, "It is as if he says, 'I don't care what you think—but I don't care what *I* think. I have a very low opinion of your opinion of me—but I have a very low opinion of *my* opinion of me.'"[4]

I saw a motivational poster with a cat looking into a mirror. It sees a lion reflecting back at itself. Across the bottom are the words, "What matters most is how you see yourself." That is the exact opposite of what God says in these verses.

The ultimate verdict concerning me is not derived from my self-image or my opinion of myself. Too often, the courtroom we live in as we go through the day is the courtroom of self. *What do I think of myself? What do I think about how I have done? How do I feel about myself?* None of those questions is as important as we think. At the end of the day, our joy and peace do not hinge on self-image, self-perception, self-evaluation, or self-esteem.

What does it look like to get out of the courtroom and escape into the joy of self-forgetfulness?

> Friends, wouldn't you want to be a person who does not need honour—nor is afraid of it? Someone who does not lust for recognition— nor, on the other hand, is frightened to death of it? Don't you want to be the kind of person who, when they see themselves in a mirror or reflected in a shop window, does not admire what they see but does not cringe either? Wouldn't you like to be the kind of person who, in their imaginary life, does not sit around fantasizing about hitting self-esteem home runs, daydreaming about successes that give them the edge over others? Wouldn't you like to be the skater who wins the silver, and yet is thrilled about those three triple jumps that the gold medal winner did? To love it the way you love a sunrise? Just to love the fact that it was done? You are as happy that they did it as if you had done it yourself. . . . This is gospel-humility, blessed self-forgetfulness.[5]

This is the kind of person we can be through the power of the gospel. It is the kind of person God is making us to be by his Spirit. You have nothing to lose in thinking of yourself less often. And you have everything to gain.

The Art of Losing Yourself

We lose ourselves when we are preoccupied and caught up in something else. We become so absorbed in something or someone outside of ourselves that we momentarily forget ourselves. Many of the things we do in life are intended to pull us outside of ourselves and usher us into the joy of losing ourselves.

C. S. Lewis once observed that love, virtue, the pursuit of knowledge, and the reception of the arts all help us escape from ourselves. By these means the soul can "correct its provincialism and heal its loneliness."[6]

We are surrounded by opportunities to abandon self-absorption and become absorbed in someone or something else. This is the art of losing yourself. Let's consider what this looks like in some of life's endeavors.

Worship

Musical worship is not centered on ourselves, but on God. Self-consciousness can appear in many forms: pursuing emotional experiences, analyzing our expressiveness, feeling awkward about singing, and focusing more on what we are doing than what *Christ* has done.

John Piper has written about how "self-consciousness kills joy and therefore kills worship."[7] He uses the example of going to the art museum. We go for the joy of seeing paintings, but if you focus on your emotions and your joy rather than the art, you ruin the experience.

The path to joy in God is not self-consciousness; it is Christ-consciousness. Worship is a gift from God when we are stuck in ourselves. This is what we were made to do—rejoice in the glories of the one who is truly glorious. Seek the Lord and experience the joy of self-forgetfulness.

Love

Loving and being loved has a unique power to pull us outside of ourselves. This is true in loving strangers, loving enemies, loving friends, and loving family. Wherever true love exists, we are escaping self.

The Song of Songs celebrates the romantic love of a couple lost in each other. Lovers fixate upon each other, describe each other, delight in each other, and praise each other. They are not constantly paralyzed by the pressure of needing to perform or meet expectations, precisely because they are not focused on self. This is God's design for intimacy in marriage. By focusing on each other and not ourselves, a relationship of assurance and fulfillment grows. We become absorbed in another. And when we are in love, all the world teems with life and beauty.

Art

The artist is a gift from God to others, and the arts play a crucial and underappreciated role in our lives. We need the artist, not because he or she is a prophetic voice of higher truth that is inaccessible to others, but because the artist possesses creative gifts that are intended to lead people to a fuller discovery of God's creativity in the world around us.

By moving past an inward focus on self, the artist helps others do the same. However, when the artist loses sight of the goal of serving others with their gifts, independence is elevated, and the artist is isolated in the experience of no longer connecting or communicating with people. Then joy is lost. Don't value self-expression above the enrichment of others. God has given you creative gifts not to take you deeper into yourself, but to draw you outside yourself.

Sports

Sports allow us to forget about ourselves. The cares of life take a backseat. The internal dialogue about self is silenced as an athlete focuses on the game at hand. Sports are a gift from God, and much of the joy of sports is the childlike joy of self-forgetfulness.

Athletes talk about being in a "zone." Those are the times we are not paralyzed by self-consciousness and are instead free to experience the thrill of competition. When we make competition all about ourselves—which is all too common among athletes—we drain the joy out of sports. But as self becomes smaller, our joy in the successes of others becomes greater. We can celebrate the beauty of the game, and our emotional state doesn't hinge entirely on our performance.

Preaching

Preachers and others who serve publicly benefit from pursuing self-forgetfulness and God-awareness. It was helpful for me, when I first started preaching, to read a caution from John Stott about the temptation to self-pre-occupation in the pulpit. His concern is that if we look at ourselves preaching in the mirror, listen to recordings of ourselves, or watch videos of ourselves, we can easily continue thinking about ourselves when we are serving. "In that case you will condemn yourself to the cramping bondage of preoccupation with yourself just at the time when, in the pulpit, it is essential to cultivate self-for-getfulness through a growing awareness of the God for whom and the people to whom you are speaking."[8]

Work

The purpose of work is to become involved in some-thing larger than ourselves. Yet we naturally place self at the center of work, approaching our jobs as a means of self-advancement, self-exaltation, and self-fulfillment. Every Monday morning we should remind ourselves that our work is not mostly about us, but about the Lord and the good of others.

Our value does not rise and fall according to status, power, or income. We reject the unhealthy ranking of working men and women that assigns value according to worldly standards and is expressed in condescending attitudes. With God, there is no partiality in connection to position and power (Ephesians 6:9). As we faithfully use our God-given abilities for his glory and the good of society, laboring in seemingly ordinary jobs, God is pleased.

Unemployment can be a great trial that leads to self-pity and self-absorption. The unemployed should continue to labor as they are able, through volunteer work or personal work, to promote the joy of self-forgetfulness.

Our Happiest Moments

John Piper has often said that no one goes to the Grand Canyon to increase their self-esteem. Think about what he says. "The really wonderful moments of joy in this world are not the moments of self-satisfaction, but self-forgetfulness. Standing on the edge of the Grand Canyon and contemplating your own greatness is pathological. At such moments we are made for a magnificent joy that comes from outside ourselves."9

Children are sometimes better at experiencing this joy than we are. It is, in fact, one of the reasons that Jesus taught his followers to become like little children (Matthew 18:3). Children generally know they are dependent and not self-sufficient, so they often look outward for help and not inward. They trust their parents. They are able to go through life remarkably carefree. We can see the joy of self-forgetfulness in them.

Of course, it's also true that young children are often self-absorbed. But they are not paralyzed by it. They may be selfish, but they don't tend to be excessively introspective. They know how to go outside of themselves. James Houston writes,

The real meaning of enjoyment is . . . the act of going outside one's self, as a small child does, to be involved with other objects for their own sake. It is therefore the antithesis of introspection, of being imprisoned within one's self. Such joy is a desire, yet it is not entrapped in self-seeking. It is a response, even an intellectual response, such as a mathematician may have to the beauty of numbers, yet it is not self-congratulatory. It is love, but not self-love; rather, it is love of everything for its own sake. Joy is akin to humility, to unconscious self-forgetfulness and to kindness in respecting the uniqueness of others.[10]

Too much introspection robs us of this joy by trapping us in ourselves. It's time to abandon self-seeking and self-absorption. It's time to move outside of ourselves. Are you ready to come alive to God's world, God's people, and God's Son? Are you ready to discover the joy of self-forgetfulness by focusing on glorious realities outside of yourself? Then here we go.

Questions for Reflection and Discussion

- What is the difference between absolute self-forgetfulness and situational self-forgetfulness?
- Can you think of a time when you experienced the joy of self-forgetfulness?

11
A World Bursting with Beauty

Awakening to the majesty of God in creation

The great preacher Charles Spurgeon experienced a considerable amount of suffering throughout his life. His wife Susannah was essentially an invalid from the time she was thirty-three years old. Because of her condition, they were unable to have more children. In addition to these challenges in the home, Spurgeon was often misrepresented and slandered in his ministry. He also suffered a number of severe physical ailments. Gout brought him constant pain.

Some of Spurgeon's greatest difficulties involved his ongoing experience of depression. He once said, "My spirits were sunken so low that I could weep by the hour like a child, and yet knew not what I wept for."[1]

Spurgeon's Surprising Remedy

There is a remedy Spurgeon personally experienced, and one he counseled others to pursue when they were downcast and depressed. It's a remedy that everyone who is inclined to unhealthy introspection is invited to experience for themselves. It is the remedy of taking in God's created world.

This doesn't mean that creation always and immediately dispels our sorrows. There is no simple cure for depression. But there are things that help. Speaking to the students in his Pastors College, Spurgeon said that "nature lies outside his window calling him to health and beckoning him to joy."

> He who forgets the humming of the bees among the heather, the cooing of the wood-pigeons in the forest, the song of birds in the woods, the rippling of rills among the rushes, and the sighing of the wind among the pines, needs not wonder if his heart forgets to sing and his soul grows heavy. . . . The ferns and the rabbits, the streams and the trouts, the fir trees and the squirrels, the primroses and the violets, the farm-yard, the new-mown hay, and the fragrant hops—these are the best medicine for hypochondriacs, the surest tonics for the declining, the best refreshments for the weary. For lack of opportunity, or inclination, these great remedies are neglected, and the student becomes a self-immolated victim.[2]

The created world has a unique way of opening our minds to the glory of God. This is why introspection is most likely to get the upper hand during the frigid months of winter, when the world is cold and gray. Don't underestimate the influence that creation, music, art, weather, leisure, love, and laughter have upon the health of the soul. There is a world waiting to be discovered and experienced.

Cornelius Plantinga observes, "The more self-absorbed we are, the less there is to find absorbing."[3] Likewise, the more we find absorbing in the world around us, the less self-absorbed we become. God draws us out of ourselves by awakening us to his majesty in the world he has made.

Do You Hear Creation's Chorus?

The nineteenth-century British poet Gerard Manley Hopkins famously wrote:

> The world is charged with the grandeur of God.
> It will flame out like shining from shook foil;
> It gathers to a greatness, like the ooze of oil.[4]

God has revealed himself in the world he has made. As Hopkins and many other poets know, sometimes it flames out, surprising us in a sudden moment of glory and beauty. Other times it oozes around us, slowly gathering to greatness that fills ordinary moments with a sense of God's presence.

Theologians call it general revelation. God's eternal power and divine nature have been clearly perceived ever since the creation of the world, in the things that have been made (Romans 1:20). Psalm 19 is a celebration of God's glory in creation. Listen to the psalmist:

> The heavens declare the glory of God,
> and the sky above proclaims his handiwork.
> Day to day pours out speech,
> and night to night reveals knowledge.
> There is no speech, nor are there words,
> whose voice is not heard.
> Their voice goes out through all the earth,
> and their words to the end of the world. (19:1–4)

This is the joyful song of creation. The witness of creation to the glory of God is not a quiet whisper, but a loud shouting. Something is being *declared*. This revelation is constant; all of creation is inundated with artistic manifestations of divine glory. It is there in the day; it is there at night. God has created a world that pulsates with his glory. This revelation of God is not vague and hidden, but clear and unmistakable. And, the voice of God in creation is universal: "Their voice goes out through all the earth, and their words to the end of the world."

Praising the Creator of All Things

In Acts 14, when Paul was in Lystra, there were pagans wanting to worship Barnabas as a god. They called him Zeus. Paul rushed into the crowd and told them to turn from living for created things and to worship the living creator God alone. He says concerning

God, "he did not leave himself without witness, for he did good by giving you rains from heaven and fruitful seasons, satisfying your hearts with food and gladness" (Acts 14:17).

God has not left himself without a witness! This is my Father's world. "The earth is the LORD's and the fullness thereof" (Psalm 24:1). "Holy, holy, holy is the LORD of hosts; the whole earth is full of his glory!" (Isaiah 6:3).

I once read that Theodore Roosevelt had a habit of staring up at the night sky with his friend. They would step outside on a clear starry night, point to the heavens, and one of them would say, "That is the Spiral Galaxy of Andromeda. It is as large as our Milky Way. It is one of a hundred million galaxies. It is seven hundred and fifty thousand light years away. It consists of one hundred billion suns, each larger than our own sun." Then there would be a pause, and then Roosevelt would grin and say, "All right, I think we feel small enough now. Good night."[5]

So, step outside. Look up at night. The stars in the midnight canopy are singing of the greatness of the power of our Lord. "He determines the number of the stars; he gives to all of them their names. Great is our Lord, and abundant in power; his understanding is beyond measure" (Psalm 147:4–5).

Rain pours down as a reminder of the kindness and severity of God: kindness, because "your Father . . . sends rain on the just and on the unjust" (Matthew 5:45); severity, because by rain he judged a rebellious world in Genesis 6–8.

The sheer number of animals and birds covering the earth proclaim his sovereignty. "For every beast of the forest is mine, the cattle on a thousand hills. I know all the birds of the hills, and all that moves in the field is mine" (Psalm 50:10–11).

And we, as humans made in God's image, are the pinnacle of creation, revealing his wisdom and glory more clearly than anything else God has made. "For you formed my inward parts; you knitted me together in my mother's womb. I praise you, for I am fearfully and wonderfully made. Wonderful are your works; my soul knows it very well" (Psalm 139:13–14).

The image of God simultaneously exalts and humbles us. We have the breathtaking privilege of reflecting God, and at the same time, we are reminded that we are not the source or the Creator. Both realities lead us to worship the sovereign Creator.

> "Worthy are you, our Lord and God,
> to receive glory and honor and power,
> for you created all things,
> and by your will they existed and were created."
> (Revelation 4:11)

Go Outside and Play

Every moment of every day, our Father is taking pleasure in the world he has made. And he intends for his children to go outside and play—that is, to use the world as a channel of grace and gladness in the Christian life and share his delight in creation. The created world can deepen our communion with God, expand our joy and thanksgiving to God, conform us further into the image of God, and encourage us to imitate God through our own creative work.

The following are a few suggestions that God can use to free us from our unhealthy introspection:

Experience "the wonder of the commonplace"

John Calvin saw the world as a grand theater of divine works. He believed there is not an atom in this universe in which you cannot see at least some brilliant sparks of God's glory.[6] He says, "There is not one blade of grass, there is no color in this world that is not intended to make us rejoice."[7] This world is endlessly fascinating, and we must not grow familiar with the countless wonders that surround us.

This is what John Piper calls "the wonder of the commonplace." He urges us toward a childlike fascination and wonder at the simple things in life.

> One of the tragedies of growing up is that we get used to things. It has its good side of course, since irritations may cease to be irritations. But there is an immense loss when we get used to the redness of the rising sun, and the roundness of the moon, and the whiteness of the snow, the wetness of the rain, the blueness of the sky, the buzzing of bumble bees, the stitching of

crickets, the invisibility of wind, the unconscious constancy of heart and diaphragm, the
weirdness of noses and ears, the number of the
grains of sand on a thousand beaches, the nev-
er-ceasing crash crash crash of countless waves,
and ten million kingly-clad flowers flourishing
and withering in woods and mountain valleys
where no one sees but God.[8]

Receive God's gifts with thanksgiving

Gratitude has a way of dispelling unhealthy
introspection.

In 1 Timothy 4, Paul is correcting a view that min-
imizes the value of physical things. He considers it "the
teaching of demons" that some "forbid marriage and
require abstinence from foods that God created to be received with thanksgiving by those who believe and know
the truth" (1 Timothy 4:1, 3). The *truth* these false teachers denied is explained in the last verse of 1 Timothy
3. The church is a pillar and buttress of the *truth*, proclaiming the message that "[Christ] was manifested in
the flesh" (1 Timothy 3:16).

These teachers, in denying the goodness of sex and
food, were denying the doctrines of creation and incarnation. Creation teaches us that "Everything created by
God is good, and nothing is to be rejected if it is received with thanksgiving" (1 Timothy 4:4). God "richly
provides us with everything to enjoy" (1 Timothy 6:17).
Likewise, the incarnation of Christ is an affirmation of

the ongoing goodness of creation. Therefore, we receive it with thanksgiving. G. K. Chesterton once said,

> You say grace before meals.
> All right.
> But I say grace before the play and the opera,
> And grace before the concert and pantomime,
> And grace before I open a book,
> And grace before sketching, painting,
> Swimming, fencing, foxing, walking, playing, dancing;
> And grace before I dip the pen in ink.[9]

Use creation to grow in godliness

We become more like Christ by observing the world God has made. Consider the following examples:

- Are you worried, fearful, and anxious? Jesus says that the presence of anxiety reveals a failure to sufficiently appreciate the lilies. "Consider the lilies of the field, how they grow: they neither toil nor spin, yet I tell you, even Solomon in all his glory was not arrayed like one of these" (Matthew 6:28–29).
- Do you struggle with laziness and sloth? "Go to the ant, O sluggard; consider her ways, and be wise" (Proverbs 6:6).
- Do you want true humility and steadfastness in suffering? The remarkable tour of creation Job experiences is what brings him to his knees, and he repents in dust and ashes (Job 38–41). One reason

we are proud is because we have yet to give sufficient thought to the ostrich (Job 39:13–18).

Value creativity and imagination

T. M. Moore bemoans the fact that "There seems to be so little celebrating of the beauty and wonder of God in creation among contemporary Christians—not much poetry, little in the way of artistic expression, few conversations or discussions, and only a trickle of music, drama, or dance celebrating the glory of God revealed in the creation around us."[10] We spend too many thoughts and too much energy on ourselves, and too little on the celebration and creation of beauty.

But Christians are those who have had their eyes opened to the glory of God. We are those who are being pulled out of ourselves, into a world charged with grandeur. We are those who know the meaning of true beauty and are being taught by the Spirit to see with new eyes. All beauty is a reminder that life is bigger than self.

I need to hear creation's chorus. I need to stop listening to myself and start listening to the God who speaks in color and stories and stars and snow and poems and his Word. I need spiritual vision from God to help me take in everyday wonders with wide-eyed delight.

Are your eyes open? Let your heart rejoice. Let your mind be stilled. Let your knees bow in reverence to the Lord. *Father, awaken my soul to see your majesty in a world bursting with beauty.*

Questions for Reflection and Discussion

- How does the world God has made pull us outside of ourselves?
- Take time to give thanks for some of God's good gifts.

12
The Gift of Community

People are God's plan to pull us outward

The themes of self and introspection appear frequently in the poetry of T. S. Eliot. For Eliot, art is far more about self-sacrifice than self-expression. He believed that self needs to be minimized for effective poetry and fruitful living.

Eliot knew that introspection is often debilitating and dangerous. He once critiqued the work of another poet by stating "he does not escape the fatal American introspectiveness; he is oversensitive and worried. He is tangled in himself."[1]

An early poem entitled "Introspection" includes a bleak image:

> The mind was six feet deep in a
> cistern and a brown snake with a tri-
> angular head having swallowed his
> tail was struggling like two fists
> interlocked.[2]

Six feet is the traditional depth of a grave. It is a picture of introspecting ourselves to death. To become introspective is to become entangled in ourselves, isolated and trapped with no way of escape. We struggle with ourselves like a deadly snake eating its own tail. Eventually, we devour ourselves spiritually, emotionally, and relationally.

"The Love Song of J. Alfred Prufrock"

One of Eliot's more popular works is "The Love Song of J. Alfred Prufrock," published in 1915.[3] It's a poem about an extremely introspective man, paralyzed by excessive self-focus. Prufrock is going to a social setting, a tea party, and he is deeply concerned about the impression he will have on those who are there—especially the women. The poem is written in such a way that the reader is unsure whether or not Prufrock ever leaves home. But one thing is certain—he never leaves self.

He considers the details of what he is wearing, how sharp and impressive he will look. But he also imagines they will say, "But how his arms and legs are thin!" Self-importance and self-criticism meet in his mind. He pictures himself descending the stairs "with a bald spot in the middle of my hair." He thinks to himself, "They will say: 'How his hair is growing thin!'"

Prufrock is nervous. He fears small talk. He wants to be full of "high sentence" and dignified speech, but he is afraid he will sound more like a fool. "It is impossible to say just what I mean!" He wants his life to sound important and exciting, but he knows his life is boring. And he fears that when he talks, others will find him boring. "I have seen the moment of my greatness flicker," he says. "And in short, I was afraid."

Poor Prufrock is so self-consumed and battered by introspection that he frets about meaningless and inconsequential things. "Shall I part my hair behind?" Because if your hair isn't done just right, people will be talking about it all week long. "Do I dare to eat a peach?" Because everyone knows there is a lot that can go wrong when a grown man attempts to eat a peach in a social setting.

The result of all this introspection is that Prufrock hides from others. He says, "I should have been a pair of ragged claws / Scuttling across the floors of the silent seas." He is like a crab, trapped in a protective shell of his own making, isolated from true community and relationships. The thing he most fears is being himself. He must not be known. So he puts up a front, a mask, so that he can feel safe and secure. Prufrock wants to sing a love song, as the title states, but he is incapable of moving beyond himself. It ends up being a song of introspection, and his relentless self-focus has made it impossible for him to truly love.

Eliot has captured something much broader than one man's experience in the character of J. Alfred Prufrock. He captures something of the condition of humanity and the tyranny of introspection.

I see myself in Prufrock. I have felt the pressure to impress. I have feared that people will find me boring. I have wondered what criticisms others may have of me. I spend too much time thinking about self.

We so easily become entangled and enslaved to ourselves. But it doesn't have to be this way.

Under a Freer Sky

Community is a gift from the crucified and risen Christ. It is not good for us to be alone (Genesis 2:18). There is freedom in getting over ourselves and in having our faults, imperfections, and sins known by others. Relationships are God's plan to move us outside of ourselves. The Spirit brings refreshment and perspective through other people.

How do we break free from the introspective bondage that ruins relationships? How do we grow in becoming less focused on ourselves and more focused on others? G. K. Chesterton points us in the right direction:

> How much happier you would be if you only knew that these people cared nothing about you! How much larger your life would be if your self could become smaller in it; if you could really look at other men with common curiosity and pleasure; if you could see them walking as they are in their sunny selfishness and their virile indifference! You would begin to be interested in them because they were not interested in you. You would break out of this tiny and tawdry theater in which your own

little plot is always being played, and you would find yourself under a freer sky, in a street full of splendid strangers.[4]

It's a painful but beautiful remedy. The Lord teaches us to die to ourselves so that we might truly live. To enjoy people, it is essential to realize that people are not thinking about you as much as you think they are. Trust me, we are not thinking about you—we are too busy thinking about ourselves! Life becomes more enjoyable as we become smaller in it and as we learn to take an interest in others.

The gospel attacks our inner Prufrock and leads us on the path of humility, love, and service in Christ. It is not enough to care about our own well-being; we must love our neighbor as we love ourselves (Matthew 22:39). It is not enough to look to our own interests; we must stop and look to the interests of others. Philippians 2:3–8 says:

> Do nothing from rivalry or conceit, but in humility count others more significant than yourselves. Let each of you look not only to his own interests, but also to the interests of others. Have this mind among yourselves, which is yours in Christ Jesus, who, though he was in the form of God, did not count equality with God a thing to be grasped, but made himself nothing, taking the form of a servant, being born in the likeness of men. And being found

in human form, he humbled himself by becoming obedient to the point of death, even death
on a cross.

This is our Savior! Jesus Christ was *consumed* with the
interests of others. He was consumed with *your* interests,
and with mine!

If Christ were looking only to his own interests, he
would never have come into this weary world to save
wretched sinners like us. He would never have left the
joyful presence of the Father in heaven to walk a lowly
path of sorrows. But he came! "Though he was rich, yet
for your sake he became poor, so that you by his poverty
might become rich" (2 Corinthians 8:9). He came not to
be served, but to serve, and to give his life as a ransom for
many (Mark 10:45).

And there is more. According to Philippians 2, this
same mind, this way of thinking, is ours in Christ Jesus.
We have been united to Christ, and therefore, his Spirit
is in us and we have been taught to give and love just as
he has given and loved.

It's true that we still think often of our own interests.
We still compare ourselves to others and wonder what
kind of impression we are making. So we still need the
command to do nothing from selfish ambition or conceit. But we have been given renewed minds that love
Christ and love others. "You yourselves have been taught
by God to love one another" (1 Thessalonians 4:9). We
have been given hearts that know the joy of losing ourselves in loving service of others. We have been swept up

into the triune love that has always existed between the Father, Son, and Holy Spirit. We have discovered the joy of self-denial.

Apart from Christ, we are trapped in that "tiny and tawdry theater" Chesterton talks about, where our "own little plot is always being played." We use people for our own ends, rather than take an interest in others and seek to bless them. But praise God, Christ has brought us out to freer skies. We now want to approach relationships in order to *give*, not to *get*. We are convinced that it truly is more blessed to give than to receive (Acts 20:35).

Life in the Church

The gift of community finds its fullest expression through membership in a local church. The way God pulls us outside of ourselves and combats our unhealthy introspection is by joining us together with other Christians.

A place of safety

The church provides a safe place to talk about the burden of introspection. Too many of us who struggle with excessive introspection never open our hearts and thoughts to others. We need people to help bear our burdens (Galatians 6:2). We need to confess our sins to others (James 5:16). But it needs to be a place of safety, a place of grace. Where do we find such relationships? Welcome to the Church of Christ, who opens her arms to the needy and the broken. Here we are free to be vulnerable.

Here we are free to open up our lives and know that we will not be rejected.

Christ alone is the one who will never disappoint us. He is the ultimate bearer of our burdens, inviting us daily to cast our cares on him. But he has taught his people by the Spirit to bear each other's burdens and to walk in love. "Two are better than one, because they have a good reward for their toil. For if they fall, one will lift up his fellow. But woe to him who is alone when he falls and has not another to lift him up!" (Ecclesiastes 4:9–10).

A place of belonging

Being part of a church reminds us that we are a part of something bigger than ourselves. The times we most want to be alone or stay home are often the times we most need the company of other believers. Through the preaching of God's Word, baptism, and the Lord's Supper, we remember that we do not live in isolation. We belong to the broader body of Christ.

Singing with other Christians is often used by God in this way. Dietrich Bonhoeffer says that when we sing among the redeemed, "It is the voice of the Church that is heard singing together. It is not you that sings, it is the Church that is singing, and you, as a member of the Church, may share in its song. Thus all singing together that is right must serve to widen our spiritual horizon."[5]

In a similar way, every "one another" command from God is a call to look outward, to move beyond introspection. In 1 Corinthians 12, we are reminded of the need we have for each other, as members of the body of

Christ. Verse 21 says, "The eye cannot say to the hand, 'I have no need of you,' nor again the head to the feet, 'I have no need of you.'" Others have gifts and strengths that God uses to compensate for what is lacking in us. What's more, in verse 26 we are told, "If one member suffers, all suffer together; if one member is honored, all rejoice together."

Don't neglect to "pray for one another" (James 5:16). Praying for others requires us to search for God's activity in their lives, in order to thank God for it. This fills us with joy. Praying for others also reminds us of the many needs of others so that we can call out to God on their behalf.

A place of service

The church provides a place to lose yourself in the joy of loving others. We can only spend so much time thinking about ourselves when we are actively serving those in need. God brings others into our lives to pull us outside of ourselves. We give. We love. We serve. We sacrifice. And as we walk this path, we discover the joy of being focused on others.

I once heard someone read a story called *The UnGiving Tree*.[6] It was inspired by and illustrated in the style of the classic children's book *The Giving Tree*. But this story, *The UnGiving Tree*, was about a tree that had so much to give, but wanted to keep all his gifts to himself. Though he had branches to climb and leaves to jump in and fruit to eat, the tree nailed a sign in to the ground that said, "Stay away!"

The story continues: "Every autumn, children would come and try to gather the trees leaves and make piles to climb and play in. And the tree would call the police. Every spring, children would try to climb up its trunk and swing from the branches. And the tree would release his pet python Larry." On that page is a lovely illustration of a python eating a little boy.

One day the tree decided it had had enough. It declared, "Never again is anyone to climb my branches or rest in my shade. My fruit and my leaves, they are MINE, MINE, MINE. And the tree took all that he had, and held it all in for months and years. And soon, hardly anyone remembered the story of the tree that had so much to give. The End." The last page has a picture of an old rotten stump.

Ah, the joy of a feel-good ending.

What is the purpose of a tree? To give. Trees give shade and fruit and syrup and furniture and firewood and paper and the oxygen we breathe and something to climb or swing from. The tree does not exist for its own selfish purposes. In the same way, it is the nature of the people of Christ to give. It is God's purpose for us to lose ourselves in the joy of loving others—to be able to say along with Paul, "I will most gladly spend and be spent for your souls" (2 Corinthians 12:15).

Through the community of the church and the ministry opportunities provided for us there, we are able to meet the needs of others. If you are lost in morbid introspection, sit down and talk to someone who is suffering—the widow who recently lost her husband, the man who has been unable to find a job for some time, the Christian with chronic pain or terminal illness. Or sit down with someone who is celebrating. This too will pull us out of ourselves, and is intended by God to bring us joy. My eyes are pried off myself as I take a genuine interest in others, give generously, practice hospitality, and do good.

It Is Grace, Nothing but Grace

I was discussing the themes of this chapter with a friend, who shared this insight about herself with me (used with permission).

I am the kind of person who would be happy to live *many* miles from the nearest neighbor. I am not naturally drawn toward people, and in certain contexts I find myself very drained—that's my introvert side, as well as my selfish preoccupation. However, even though my personality hasn't changed, I am much freer today than I was even ten years ago, as the Lord has been faithful to minimize my significance to myself and increase the significance of others—to their benefit and my own.

The more I see my sin and weaknesses, the more I recognize that people are essential to my ability to glorify Christ. I am more drawn to others now because I know my need, *our* need, and that trumps personality preferences and self-preoccupation. The body of Christ is a beautiful thing, and one we need to see our part in—be it minuscule or grand.

Be encouraged. God is at work in us. It is not uncommon for introspective people to want to avoid others. But God gives community as a gift. If we approach relationships with an introspective orientation, we squander the gift. The fruit of the Spirit is love, and through love we steward the gift.

There are some who are alone and through sickness, persecution, or missionary work are not able to experience the gift of community as we do. God in his loving sovereignty will care for their every need. But those of us who have the gift of friends, the gift of belonging, and the gift of gathering ought to thank God for this provision. Bonhoeffer writes,

> The physical presence of other Christians is a source of incomparable joy and strength to the believer. . . . Therefore, let him who until now has had the privilege of living a common Christian life with other Christians praise God's grace from the bottom of his heart. Let him thank God on his knees and declare: It is grace, nothing but grace, that we are allowed to live in community with Christian brethren.[7]

Yes, let us thank God for community. Let us praise the Lord for the ways he has used others in the past to pull us outside of ourselves, and for how he will continue to do so in the future. It is grace, nothing but grace.

Questions for Reflection and Discussion

- How does the local church help relieve the burden of introspection?
- In your experience, how have relationships pulled you outside of yourself?

13
Ten Looks

We were made for Christ-exalting extra-spection

When I was a teenager, I went through a miserable phase where I was self-absorbed and bored by everything. I know what you're thinking: *We all did that as teenagers.* Maybe, but there are ways I took things to the next level.

Wherever my family went, whether family vacations, family reunions, or visiting friends, I stayed in the van by myself. I didn't have keys to the van, and it wasn't running. No heat. No air conditioning. No music. But I stayed there for hours on end. The winter days were pretty cold. Summer was bearable if you kept a few doors open and dressed appropriately. I wasn't doing anything in particular in the van—just sleeping or staring at the ground. Stewing in teenage angst, I guess.

One summer my parents saved up and took the family on a vacation to the western states. That was unusual for us. We lived in Pennsylvania, and it was the only time I remember flying to get to our vacation destination. It was a once-in-a-lifetime kind of experience.

There were incredible views and amazing national parks. One place we went included a breathtaking outlook at Jenny Lake in Wyoming. It is a magnificent, clear blue lake, with the awe-inspiring Grand Teton Mountains towering in the background and reflecting in full color off the lake. It is truly amazing.

Or so I've been told.

Confession: I've actually only seen the postcard. Why? Because I stayed in the van.

I remember my parents appealing to me to get out of the van and walk the twenty or thirty yards necessary on that beautiful summer day so that I could take in this glorious, panoramic view. But I was entirely disinterested. Somehow the van won that day.

This is what introspection is like.

Get Out of the Van

There is a world of beauty outside the van. By looking outward and upward, we behold our God. But introspection says "No thanks. I'm going to sit in the van." God, therefore, comes to us in Christ and graciously calls us to get out of the van. He lifts up our eyes. He empowers us to see the greatness of his love for us in Christ. He is calling us now. He invites us to get out of the van and take in the privileges of his grace, the glory of Christ, and the hope of heaven.

The gospel leads us outside of ourselves. Comparatively speaking, there are not many calls in Scripture to look at ourselves. But again and again, we are called to lift our eyes to the Lord, to behold him, and to set our minds and hearts on him.

Sinclair Ferguson says, "The evangelical orientation is inward and subjective. We are far better at looking inward than we are at looking outward. Instead, we need to expend our energies admiring, exploring, expositing, and extolling Jesus Christ."[1] In contrast to this inward orientation, John Newton wrote of being swallowed up in contemplating Christ: "To stand at the foot of it [the cross], with a softened heart and melting eyes; to forget our sins, sorrows, and burdens, while we are wholly swallowed up in the contemplation of him who bore our sins in his own body upon the tree; is certainly the most desirable situation on this side of the grave."[2]

The Glory of Christ

The Christian life is a life of radical extra-spection. For every look to ourselves, we should be taking ten looks to Christ. And every time we look at ourselves, what we see should lead us back to Christ. Any sin we find should drive us to the work of Christ *for us*. And any good we find in ourselves should reveal the work of Christ *in us* and *through us*. Any weakness we find should lead us to the power of Christ *toward us*.

Christ is all in all. He invites us to look to him at all times. He commands it—and could there possibly be a more gracious command?

The Christian life is lived as we set our minds on the one to whom we have been united. Christ is your life.

The essence of the Christian life is 1 Peter 1:8: "Though you have not seen him, you love him. Though you do not now see him, you believe in him and rejoice with joy that is inexpressible and filled with glory."

The message we refuse to move on from is the good news of "the unsearchable riches of Christ" (Ephesians 3:8). There are not many riches in us, and we quickly reach the end of what can be said about ourselves. But the riches of Christ have no end. His glory is unsearchable. His beauty is unfathomable. His power is incomparable. His grace surpasses knowledge.

"We have seen his glory, glory as of the only Son from the Father, full of grace and truth" (John 1:14). "Full of grace and truth"—what a Savior! He is the one who loves us and has freed us from our sins by his blood! He is the Alpha and the Omega, who is and who was and who is to come! The Christian has no choice—we gladly resolve to know nothing except Jesus Christ and him crucified (1 Corinthians 2:2). "Indeed, I count everything as loss because of the surpassing worth of knowing Christ Jesus my Lord. For his sake I have suffered the loss of all things and count them as rubbish, in order that I may gain Christ" (Philippians 3:8).

There is a fountain of glory that will never run dry. Taste and see that the Lord is good. Jesus Christ is more excellent than the most breathtaking sunset, the most brilliant painting, the most stunning performance. Every earthly beauty pales in comparison to the beauty of the Lord of Glory. And the more we look to him and learn of him, the more we discover how little of his love and power and beauty we really know.

This is a truth that the Puritans understood, and one which has been largely lost in our day. They have volumes and volumes of sermons on Christ.

- Isaac Ambrose wrote more than six hundred pages (in a rather small font!) full of Christ in *Looking unto Jesus*.
- Thomas Goodwin devoted volume 5 of his works to the sacrifice of Christ and his work as mediator.
- *The Works of John Owen, volume 1*, is on the glory of Christ. (It would be good for some who spend a lot of time in volume 6 of his *Works*, on sin and temptation, to give the same attention to volume 1.)
- John Flavel wrote *The Fountain of Life opened up: or, A Display of Christ in his essential and mediatorial glory. Containing forty-two sermons.* A few years ago I read dozens of those sermons out loud as morning devotions with a group of friends.
- Robert Asty wrote *Rejoicing in the Lord Jesus in All Cases and Conditions* to help us fix our eyes on Christ.

If the Puritans are not your cup of tea, a number of contemporary books aim at the same goal. A few of my favorites that are not too long include *Rejoicing in Christ* by Michael Reeves, *Seeing and Savoring Jesus Christ* by John Piper, *Living the Cross Centered Life* by C. J. Mahaney,

Who Is Jesus? by Greg Gilbert, and *The Cross He Bore* by Frederick Leahy. Longer books that are well worth your time include *Knowing Christ* by Mark Jones, and *The Cross of Christ* by John Stott.

Lay Aside Every Weight

The writer of Hebrews describes the Christian life as a race that is run *looking to Jesus*.

> Therefore, since we are surrounded by so great a cloud of witnesses, let us also lay aside every weight, and sin which clings so closely, and let us run with endurance the race that is set before us, looking to Jesus, the founder and perfecter of our faith, who for the joy that was set before him endured the cross, despising the shame, and is seated at the right hand of the throne of God.
>
> Consider him who endured from sinners such hostility against himself, so that you may not grow weary or fainthearted (Hebrews 12:1–3).

There is a race set before us with a great cloud of witnesses. There is an astounding mass of people, expanding as far as the eye can see. It includes the saints recorded in Hebrews 11, as a strengthening reminder that we are not alone.

Although they are watching us, the emphasis is not so much on what they see in us as it is what we see in them. These men and women are witnesses. They have gone before us. They have fought the good fight, they have finished the race, and they have kept the faith. Was it because they were stronger or better than us? No, they too were weak. They too knew trials of many kinds. They too shed tears.

The "Therefore" of Hebrews 12:1 contains tremendous encouragement for weary, lonely, and troubled souls today. No temptation seizes us that has not already been faced *and overcome* by those who have gone before. Believers in every age have faced the same fear and unbelief. And they triumphed by faith in Christ. They faced the same discouragements, the same pull toward unhealthy introspection. And they are more than conquerors through him who loves us. They are not merely examples of faith; they are reminders of the faithfulness of God to his own.

In this race we are to "lay aside every weight, and sin which clings so closely." Some people think that looking to Christ means there is no mortification of sin, no *putting off* required. But Scripture says this work is a daily necessity because we are so easily entangled.

"Every weight" certainly includes the weight of excessive introspection. Not every weight is a sin. But every weight is to be thrown aside. If introspection is weighing you down, get rid of it. Athletes throw off excessive clothes, which would otherwise encumber. Christians throw off excessive introspection, which also encumbers us in the race God has called us to.

To look to Christ as we ought, we must lay aside certain weights too. These include:

- The weight of *ego*, which will only lead to the smugness of a fulfilled pride or the self-pity of an unfulfilled pride
- The weight of *vanity*, which will only lead to self-love or self-hatred
- The weight of *false guilt*, which will only breed discouragement and rob us of joy
- The weight of *comparison*, which will only take our eyes off Christ and the finish line and place them on others
- The weight of *condemnation*, which will only slow us down by keeping our focus on our guilt and denying the finished work of Christ for us

Lay aside *every weight*, and run.

Looking to Jesus

Most importantly, we must run the race *looking to Jesus*. At this point even the crowd fades into the background. They only serve to point our attention to Christ anyway, because they are followers of him and witnesses to him. Our sin fades into the background as well, because we are *looking to Jesus*. We are not to be oriented primarily toward the struggle or toward our sin. We are oriented to Christ. We turn our eyes away from everything and everyone else, and we look to him alone.

Looking to Jesus means our hearts and minds are resolutely fixed on him. We think about him, we rejoice in him, we rely upon him, we love and follow him. Forget yourself. Forget others. Forget everything that is seen. "We look not to the things that are seen but to the things that are unseen" (2 Corinthians 4:18). "If then you have been raised with Christ, seek the things that are above, where Christ is, seated at the right hand of God. Set your minds on things that are above, not on things that are on earth" (Colossians 3:1–2). Look to Jesus.

To look to him is to consider who he is and what he has done. Who is he, according to Hebrews 12:2?

He is the pioneer and perfecter of our faith.

We run with a faith that has its source in him. And, we have the sure promise of God that he will bring our faith to completion. I am not the one who perfects my faith or keeps myself to the end. Jesus does! He not only creates our faith; he completes it.

He is the one who acts with joy in view.

All that Christ did for our salvation was motivated by the joy set before him. In suffering, he remembered the goal . . . the outcome, the future. And because we are united to him, we too have an unshakable joy set before us. The Christian hope is *prospective* or forward-looking, not *introspective* or inward-looking.

This hope reminds us that one day sorrow, death, and pain will be no more, "for the former things have passed away" (Revelation 21:4). One day sin will no longer cling closely. One day we will rise. One day we will stand before the glorious and majestic one, in whose presence there is fullness of joy and pleasures forevermore. We look now by faith to the one we will one day look upon face-to-face.

He is the one who endured the cross.

His very name is a reminder that he came to save his people from their sins (Matthew 1:21). In enduring the cross, he endured the wrath of God against sin. The Savior bleeds. The sovereign one dies. "Christ redeemed us from the curse of the law by becoming a curse for us" (Galatians 3:13). He not only *has saved us* from the *penalty* of sin, he also *is saving us* from the *power* of sin and he *will one day save us* fully from the *presence* of sin. All of this was secured in his death. Looking to Jesus always centers on looking to the cross he endured. He was cursed that we might be blessed beyond our wildest imaginations.

He is the one who despised the shame.

There was unspeakable shame associated with the cross. The Lord of Glory was mocked and spit upon. His friends abandoned him. His reputation was disgraced. Shame surrounded him.

What did our Lord do? He *despised* the shame. He considered the great shame of the cross as nothing, as a waste and distraction, compared to the greater joy that awaited him. In despising the shame of the cross, he paved the way for us to triumph over shame.

> "Fear not, for you will not be ashamed;
> be not confounded, for you will not be disgraced;

for you will forget the shame of your youth,
and the reproach of your widowhood you will remember no more.
For your Maker is your husband,
the LORD of hosts is his name;
and the Holy One of Israel is your Redeemer,
the God of the whole earth he is called."
(Isaiah 54:4–5)

Jesus is the one who sat down.

"After making purification for sins, he sat down at the right hand of the Majesty on high" (Hebrews 1:3). He sat down, and he remains seated.

Of all the uncertainties in life, this is certain—the King of Love is on his throne. And, to the glory of his name, he will bring us safely home. We are secure in him because we are seated in heaven, where Christ is. Therefore, when we look to him, we remember not only what he *has* done for us, but what he *is* doing and what he *will* do when he returns.

Hope for the Weary

In college, I sometimes went running with Meghan, who is now my wife. She was a very serious runner—a cross-country All-American in college—and I figured she would be looking to marry a runner. So I decided I would run with her to attempt to woo her with my extraordinary athletic prowess.

Meghan did seven-mile training runs like it was a walk in the park. As we took off on our run, Meghan was cruising along, talking to me. After a couple of miles, she noticed that I was panting rather heavily and apparently the color was draining from my face. "Jared, are you feeling okay?" Of course, I said yes. I would have rather fallen over dead than tell the girl of my dreams that I was struggling to keep up with her.

After pushing myself as hard as I could for some time, Meghan said, "Jared, you don't look good at all. Do you need to stop running?" She suggested I stay put while she did a few more miles and looped back around. I reluctantly agreed. My body didn't really give me a choice in the matter.

When she was out of sight, I collapsed by the side of the road. While I lay there, I threw up and continued to feel worse. Meghan eventually came back and saw that I was in no condition to run. She asked if I would like her to run back to get the car and come back to pick me up. I said yes. So my efforts to impress turned into a Good Samaritan moment where she pulled up to the side of the road, helped this pathetic guy into the car, and drove me home.

In Hebrews 12 we are encouraged to run with endurance. The Christian life is not a sprint; it is a long-distance race. And weariness is common along the way.

"Let us run with *endurance*." We know to expect weights, sins, and hardship as we run the great Christian race. When we find ourselves weary, tempted to give up, burdened by introspection or any other weight, how have we gotten there? It is because we have failed to sufficiently consider him. Hebrews 12:3 says "Consider him . . . *so that* you may not grow weary or fainthearted."

Apart from a focused consideration of Christ, we will grow weary and lose heart. But in Christ there is strength and help in time of need. He is our "hiding place from the wind, a shelter from the storm, like streams of water in a dry place, like the shade of a great rock in a weary land" (Isaiah 32:2). Jesus is the true King David, so that everyone who is in distress, everyone who is in debt, and everyone who is discontented can gather to him (1 Samuel 22:2).

When strength is failing in the race—and strength will fail us at times—we must call our souls to him once again: *Consider him!* Consider Christ in all the Scriptures. Consider his person and work. Consider his offices as prophet, priest, and king. Consider his character, his life, his deeds, his death, his resurrection, his reign. *Consider him!*

Sing songs that will help you consider him. Listen to sermons and read books that are full of him. Join a church that is committed more than anything to helping people look to Jesus and treasure him.

Looking to Christ is not only a sight that brings joy; it is also a sight that transforms. Beholding his glory not only makes our souls happy, but it is the best and surest way to make our souls holy. "And we all, with unveiled face, beholding the glory of the Lord, are being transformed into the same image from one degree of glory to another" (2 Corinthians 3:18).

May the Lord Direct Your Heart

The great benedictions of Scripture send us into life in the real world, armed with an accurate knowledge of who we are, but sustained by fixing our eyes not on ourselves, but on Christ. One of the benedictions relevant to those stuck looking inward is found in 2 Thessalonians 3:5. "May the Lord direct your hearts to the love of God and to the steadfastness of Christ."

This is my prayer for all who read this book. More importantly, it is the heart of your Father for you.

What is your heart set on? Where are your affections and your attention directed? A heart directed to self is a heart missing out on the glories of Christ for which we were made. Let's pray that God would redirect our hearts away from self.

"May the Lord direct your hearts to the love of God and to the steadfastness of Christ."

Remember the love of God.

The love of God for us remains when we are at our worst. This great love is revealed in the substitutionary death of Christ for sinners. "For God so loved the world, that he gave his only Son" (John 3:16). "God shows his love for us in that while we were still sinners, Christ died for us" (Romans 5:8). "In this the love of God was made manifest among us, that God sent his only Son into the world, so that we might live through him. In this is love, not that we have loved God but that he loved us and sent his Son to be the propitiation for our sins" (1 John 4:9–10).

May the Lord direct your hearts to the love of God. May his redeeming love be the eternal song of your soul. May you rest in the security of knowing you are deeply loved.

Remember the steadfastness of Christ.

We are not steadfast. We often waver and fail. Our eyes turn inward; emotions take over, and we are tempted to lose heart. But Jesus Christ is always steadfast. Even when our eyes drift from him, his eyes remain fixed upon us in love. When our hearts wander from him, his heart remains set on us. When we are tempted to give up, he assures us that he will never give up on us. And because the object of our faith is steadfast, unchanging, and faithful, we are strengthened for the race and made steadfast as we look to him.

Therefore, lay aside every weight. Look to Jesus. Run with endurance. Consider him.

> "May the Lord direct your hearts to the love of God and to the steadfastness of Christ."
> (2 Thessalonians 3:5)

Questions for Reflection and Discussion

- What aspect of Christ's glory in Hebrews 12:1–3 encourages you today?
- Share a Scripture that has helped you treasure Christ and look to him.

Acknowledgments

I am indebted to Barbara Juliani and New Growth Press for the opportunity to be published, and for the excellence they bring to their work.

My writing group at Covenant Fellowship Church prayed for me, met with me, and gave me feedback. Friends in the church shared their experience of introspection with me. The elders of Covenant Fellowship Church contribute greatly to any usefulness I have in ministry through their care, encouragement, gifting, and prayers.

Several pastor-friends took time to read my first manuscript and offer feedback. Thanks to Jon Payne, Tim Kerr, and Joel Shorey.

My wife, Meghan, helped me find the time to write this book. She also read chapters out loud to me. And she always knows how to help me when my mind is stuck on me.

Adam and Bethany Sacks model the lack of self-absorption I aspire to. They are the best friends a guy could ask for.

My dad is a faithful father, pastor, and friend. He has invested in me in countless ways. My dear mother gave me a massive list of copy edits. She tells me I am the best author in the whole wide world, and she doesn't understand how anyone could possibly be critical of anything I do.

David Powlison's teaching at the 2007 Sovereign Grace Pastors Conference was a great help to me in battling unhealthy introspection. Sinclair Ferguson, Ray Ortlund Jr., John Newton, and Richard Sibbes have had a profound impact on my understanding of grace. Dave Harvey kindly and sacrificially mentored me in ministry, seeing grace where natural eyes would see only inexperience.

Marty Machowski encouraged me to write and introduced me to a publisher. Justin Taylor met with me for lunch a few years back to talk about writing. Mike McKinley and Stephen Altrogge took time on the phone to answer my questions about writing and publishing.

Thanks everyone!

Endnotes

Chapter 1

1. D. Martyn Lloyd-Jones, *Spiritual Depression: Its Causes and Its Cure* (Grand Rapids, MI: Eerdmans, 1965), 103.

2. Ibid., 88.

3. C. H. Spurgeon, "Eyes Right," Sermon No. 2058, http://www.biblebb.com/files/spurgeon/2058.htm.

4. Ibid.

5. Andrew A. Bonar, *Memoir and Remains of the R. M. M'Cheyne* (Edinburgh: The Banner of Truth Trust, 1966), 293.

6. David Powlison, "In the Last Analysis: Look Out for Introspection" (presented at the Sovereign Grace Leaders Conference, April 13, 2007).

Chapter 2

1. Anthony A. Hoekema, *Created in God's Image* (Grand Rapids, MI: Eerdmans, 1986), 110.

2. Richard Lints, *Identity and Idolatry: The Image of God and Its Inversion*, New Studies in Biblical Theology (Downers Grove, IL: InterVarsity Press, 2015), 11.

3. David F. Wells, *The Courage to Be Protestant: Truth-Lovers, Marketers, and Emergents in the Postmodern World* (Grand Rapids, MI: Eerdmans, 2008), 137.

4. Ibid., 153ff.

5. Ibid., 161.

6. John Calvin, *Institutes of the Christian Religion*, 1.1.1, ed. John T. McNeill, trans. Ford Lewis Battles (Philadelphia: Westminster Press), 1960.

7. Ibid., 1.1.2.

8. John Calvin, "Commentary on Isaiah 6:5," http://www.sacred-texts.com/chr/calvin/cc13/cc13012.htm.

9. Thomas Chalmers, "Essay on Guthrie's The Christian's Great Interest: Part I," http://graceonlinelibrary.org/salvation/sanctification/essay-on-guthries-the-christians-great-interest-part-i-by-thomas-chalmers.

10. Ibid.

11. Francis A. Schaeffer, *The Francis A. Schaeffer Trilogy, Book One: The God Who Is There* (Wheaton, IL: Crossway Books, 1990), 103.

12. Herman Ridderbos, *Paul: An Outline of His Theology* (Grand Rapids, MI: Eerdmans Publishing Co., 1975), 272.

13. Jonathan Edwards, *The Works of Jonathan Edwards*, Vol. Two (Edinburgh: The Banner of Truth Trust, 1974), 619.

Chapter 3

1. "Wikipedia: Ten things you may not know about Wikipedia," Wikipedia.org, https://en.wikipedia.org/wiki/Wikipedia:Ten_things_you_may_not_know_about_Wikipedia.

2. Melanie Hall, "Family albums fade as the young put only themselves in picture," *Telegraph*, June 13, 2013, http://www.telegraph.co.uk/technology/news/10123875/Family-albums-fade-as-the-young-put-only-themselves-in-picture.html.

3. "The Oxford Dictionaries Word of the Year 2013 Is 'Selfie,'" Oxford Dictionaries, http://blog.oxforddictionaries.com/2013/11/word-of-the-year-2013-winner.

4. Jillian McHugh, "'Selfies' just as much for the insecure as show-offs," *Bunbury Mail*, April 3, 2013, http://www.bunburymail.com.au/story/1407035/selfies-just-as-much-for-the-insecure-as-show-offs.

5. Rachel Hills, "Ugly Is the New Pretty: How Unattractive Selfies Took Over the Internet," *New York Magazine*, http://nymag.com/thecut/2013/03/ugly-is-the-new-pretty-a-rise-in-gross-selfies.html.

6. Heidi Grant Halvorson, "To Succeed, Forget Self-Esteem," *Harvard Business Review*, September 20, 2012, https://hbr.org/2012/09/to-succeed-forget-self-esteem.html.

7. Jon Bloom, "Lay Aside the Weight of Low Self-Image," desiringgod.org, December 7, 2015, http://www.desiringgod.org/articles/lay-aside-the-weight-of-low-self-image.

8. Ibid.

9. Timothy Keller, *Gospel in Life Study Guide: Grace Changes Everything* (Grand Rapids, MI: Zondervan, 2010), 16.

Chapter 4

1. Nathaniel Hawthorne, *The Scarlet Letter* (Pleasantville, NY: The Reader's Digest Association Inc., 1984), 99.

2. Ibid., 100.

3. J. I. Packer, *A Quest for Godliness: The Puritan Vision of the Christian Life* (Wheaton, IL: Crossway Books, 1990), 118.

4. Thomas Hooker, *The Poor Doubting Christian Drawn to Christ* (Keyser, WV: Odom Publications, 1991), 59.

5. This insight is from John Piper. *Ask Pastor John*, May 5, 2015. "Have I Cast My Anxieties or Hoarded Them?" http://www.desiringgod.org/interviews/have-i -cast-my-anxieties-or-hoarded-them.

6. John Newton, *The Works of John Newton, Vol. 2: Cardiphonia (Continued)*, Letter VII (Edinburgh: The Banner of Truth Trust, 2015), 15.

7. C. H. Spurgeon, *The Treasury of David, Vol. Three* (Peabody, MA: Hendrickson Publishers, 2014), 39, 47.

8. J. C. Ryle, *The Upper Room: Biblical Truths for Modern Times* (New Kensington, PA: Whitaker House, 2015), 272.

Chapter 5

1. Richard Sibbes, "There is a depth of mercy deeper than any misery or rebellion of ours," *The Works of Richard Sibbes*, Vol. 3 (Edinburgh: The Banner of Truth Trust, 1983), 36.

2. Os Guinness, *God in the Dark: The Assurance of Faith Beyond a Shadow of Doubt* (Wheaton, IL: Crossway Books, 1996), 139.

3. John Owen, *The Works of John Owen, Vol. 2: Communion with God* (Edinburgh: The Banner of Truth Trust, 1965), 239.

Chapter 6

1. David E. Prince, "The Accuser in the Mirror: The Danger of False Guilt," https://erlc.com/article/the-accuser-in-the-mirror-the-danger-of-false-guilt.

2. Lou Priolo, *Self-Image: How to Overcome Inferiority Judgments, Resources for Biblical Living* (Phillipsburg, NJ: P&R Publishing, 2007), 7–8.

3. Newton, *Works, Vol. 2: Cardiphonia*, 29.

4. Paul David Tripp, *Instruments in the Redeemer's Hands: People in Need of Change Helping People in Need of Change* (Phillipsburg, NJ: P&R Publishing, 2002), 250.

Chapter 7

1. Nancy Wilson, *The Fruit of Her Hands: Respect and the Christian Woman* (Moscow, ID: Canon Press, 1997), 69–70.

2. Ibid., 70–71.

3. C. H. Spurgeon, *C.H. Spurgeon Autobiography: The Early Years*, Vol. 1 (Edinburgh: The Banner of Truth Trust, 1962), 104.

4. C. S. Lewis, *The Inspirational Writings of C. S. Lewis: Surprised by Joy, Reflections on the Psalms, the Four Loves, the Business of Heaven* (New York: Inspirational Press 1994), 120.

5. J. I. Packer and Carolyn Nystrom, *Praying: Finding Our Way through Duty to Delight* (Downers Grove, IL: InterVarsity Press, 2006), 125.

6. William Bridge, *A Lifting Up for the Downcast* (Edinburgh: The Banner of Truth Trust, 1961), 82.

Chapter 8

1. Richard Sibbes, *The Complete Works of Richard Sibbes, Vol. 2: Bowels Opened (Sermons on the Song of Solomon 4–6)*, 30.

2. Sam Storms and Justin Taylor, eds., *For the Fame of God's Name: Essays in Honor of John Piper* (Wheaton, IL: Crossway, 2010), 279.

3. Newton, *Works, Vol. 2: Cardiphonia*, 33.

4. Calvin, *Institutes*, 3.14.18.

5. J. C. Ryle, *Holiness: Its Nature, Hindrances, Difficulties, and Roots* (Darlington: Evangelical Press, 1979), 228.

Chapter 9

1. Thomas Wilcox and Horatius Bonar, *Christ Is All,*

and Saving Faith Discovered (Edinburgh: Johnstone and Hunter, 1855), 18–19. The quote is one of Bonar's footnotes on Thomas Wilcox's famous sermon, "Honey Out of the Rock," or "Christ Is All."

2. Arthur G. Bennett, compiler, *The Valley of Vision: A Collection of Puritan Prayers & Devotions* (Edinburgh: The Banner of Truth Trust, 1975), 70.

3. B. B. Warfield, *The Works of Benjamin B. Warfield*, Vol. 7, Perfectionism, Part One (Grand Rapids, MI: Baker Book House, 2003), 90.

4. Ibid., 90, 114.

5. Jerry Bridges, *Respectable Sins: Confronting the Sins We Tolerate* (Colorado Springs: NavPress, 2007), 37.

6. John Stott, *Christian Basics* (Grand Rapids, MI: Eerdmans, 1969), 121–22.

7. C. H. Spurgeon, "The Exceeding Riches of His Grace," from *Metropolitan Tabernacle Pulpit*, Vol. 28 (Pasadena, TX: Pilgrim Publications, 1986), 344–45.

Chapter 10

1. Helen Keller, *The Story of My Life*, http://www.afb.org/mylife/book.asp?ch=P1Ch22.

2. Timothy Keller, *The Freedom of Self-Forgetfulness: The Path to True Christian Joy* (Chorley, England: 10Publishing, 2012), 32.

3. Ibid.

4. Ibid., 26.

5. Ibid., 34–35.

6. C. S. Lewis, *An Experiment in Criticism* (Cambridge: Cambridge University Press, 1961), 138.

7. John Piper, *Desiring God: Meditations of a Christian Hedonist* (Sisters, OR: Multnomah Publishers, Inc., 1986), 95.

8. John R. W. Stott, *Between Two Worlds: The Art of Preaching in the Twentieth Century* (Grand Rapids, MI: Eerdmans, 1982), 272.

9. John Piper, *Don't Waste Your Life* (Wheaton, IL: Crossway, 2003), 33–34.

10. James M. Houston, *The Creator: Living Well in God's World, Vol. 4, Soul's Longing* (Colorado Springs: David C. Cook, 2007), 223.

Chapter 11

1. Quoted by John Piper in *Battling Unbelief: Defeating Sin with Superior Pleasure* (Sisters, OR: Multnomah Books, 2007), 122.

2. C. H. Spurgeon, *Lectures to My Students* (Pasadena, TX: Pilgrim Publications, 1990), 172.

3. Cornelius Plantinga Jr., *Not the Way It's Supposed to Be: A Breviary of Sin* (Grand Rapids, MI: Eerdmans Publishing Co., 1995), 122.

4. Gerard Manley Hopkins, "God's Grandeur," *Selected Poems of Gerard Manley Hopkins* (Mineola, NY: Dover Publications, Inc.), 20.

5. Steve DeWitt, *Eyes Wide Open: Enjoying God in Everything* (Grand Rapids, MI: Credo House Publishers, 2012), 36.

6. Calvin, *Institutes*, 1.5.1.

7. Quoted by Kimberly Garza, *It Was Good: Making Art to the Glory of God, Revised and Expanded*, ed. Ned Bustard (Baltimore, MD: Square Halo Books, 2006), 208.

8. John Piper, *The Pleasures of God: Meditations on God's Delight in Being God* (Sisters, OR: Multnomah Publishers, Inc., 2000), 96.

9. G. K. Chesterton, "A Grace," *The Collected Works of G. K. Chesterton: Collected Poetry* (San Francisco, CA: Ignatius Press, 1994), 43.

10. T. M. Moore, *Consider the Lilies: A Plea for Creational Theology* (Phillipsburg, NJ: P&R Publishing, 2005), 96.

Chapter 12

1. T. S. Eliot, "Introspection," *The Poems of T. S. Eliot, Vol. 1: Collected and Uncollected Poems* (London: Faber & Faber, 2015), 1162.

2. Ibid., 273.

3. Ibid., 5–9.

4. G. K. Chesterton, *Heretics/Orthodoxy* (Nashville: Thomas Nelson, Inc., 2000), 181.

5. Dietrich Bonhoeffer, *Life Together: The Classic Exploration of Christian Community* (New York: Harper & Row Publishers, Inc., 1954), 61.

6. As told in *For the Life of the World: Letters to the Exiles* DVD, video series created by Action Institute and produced by Gorilla Pictures (2014).

7. Bonhoeffer, *Life Together*, 19–20.

Chapter 13

1. Quoted by C. J. Mahaney, *Living the Cross Centered Life: Keeping the Gospel the Main Thing* (Sisters, OR: Multnomah Publishers, 2009), 40.

2. Newton, *Works, Vol. 2: Cardiphonia*, 47.

Printed in Great Britain
by Amazon

44536842R00109